Cine Cameras

John Wade

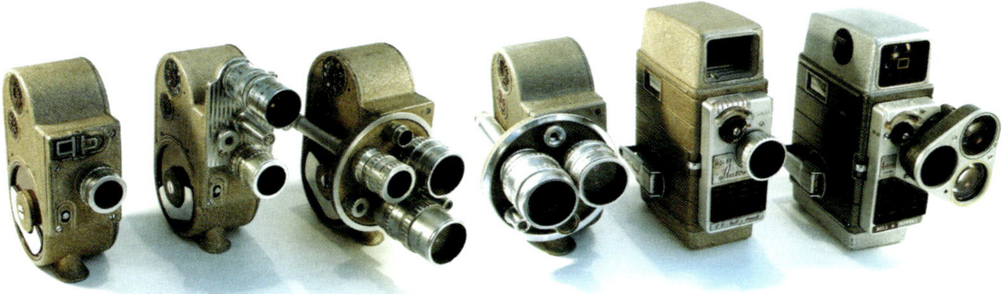

Throughout the 1950s Bell & Howell produced a huge variety of cameras in varying styles. Pictured here from that decade are the single-lens 605A, twin-lens 605B, triple-lens 605C, twin-lens Viceroy, Autoset and Autoset Turret.

A Shire book

Published in 2004 by Shire Publications Ltd,
Cromwell House, Church Street, Princes Risborough,
Buckinghamshire HP27 9AA, UK.
(Website: www.shirebooks.co.uk)

British Library Cataloguing in Publication Data:
Wade, John.
Cine cameras. – (Shire album; 429)
1. Cameras – History
2. Motion pictures cameras – History
I. Title 771.3'2
ISBN 0 7478 0592 X.

Cover: *Centre is a 9.5 mm Pathé Baby. Clockwise from top left are a Movinette 8B, made by Zeiss Ikon; a 16 mm Keystone Criterion; a Revere Ranger-8 camera fitted with an Elgeet Synchronex 8 lens and meter; and a Bolex H16.*

ACKNOWLEDGEMENTS

The following photographs are © Christie's: pages 7, 9 (both), 10 (both), 13 (top), 20 (middle), 42 (bottom), 43 (top), 46 (top). Christie's is the world's leading auction house, handling collectable and vintage cameras, movie equipment and memorabilia. (For more information please visit: www.christies.com/cameras) The following pictures are reproduced by kind permission of Arri (UK) Limited: pages 38 (both), 41 (bottom), 46 (bottom left). Other photographs are acknowledged as follows: page 12, kindly supplied by Alan Acres; page 46 (bottom right), by courtesy of Panavision; page 37 (bottom), by Dieter Scheiba; page 5, by Bob White. The photograph on page 6 (bottom) first appeared in *Moving Pictures: How They Are Made and Worked*, first published in 1912. All other pictures are from the author's own camera collection and picture library.

Printed in Great Britain by CIT Printing Services Ltd, Press Buildings, Merlins Bridge, Haverfordwest, Pembrokeshire SA61 1XF.

Contents

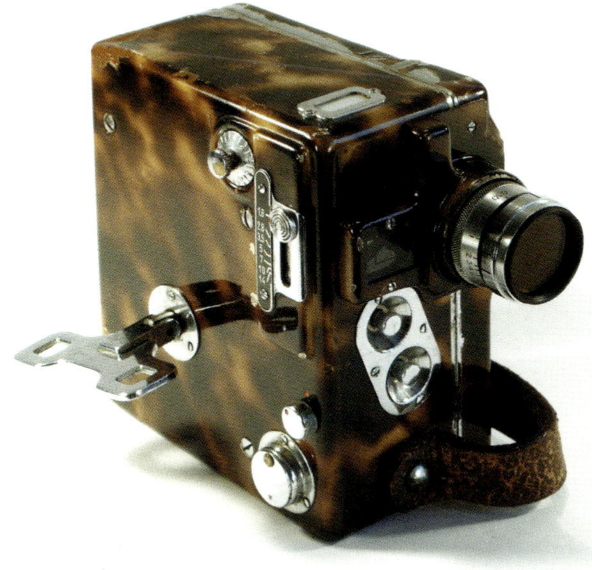

Ditmar was an Austrian company that produced cameras in all the popular gauges. This 9.5 mm model from 1936 is rare today for having the tortoiseshell finish that was available as an extra.

Introduction

At the cinema, the fact that a moving picture can be perceived as such relies on the image of an object remaining in the brain for a split second after that object has been removed from the viewer's line of sight. So a series of still pictures, each showing an individual snippet of progressive action, when viewed at speed will give the illusion of a single, moving image.

This phenomenon, known as 'persistence of vision', was noted as far back as the eleventh century by the Arab astronomer Al Hazen. Much later, in the 1820s, persistence of vision devices that used artwork for their effect became popular. But it was not until the advent of early photographic processes that all this came together to produce equipment capable of what was then known as 'animated photography'. It marked the start of a new breed of camera, used by professional cinematographers and amateur film makers alike.

The development of these cine cameras, the similarities and sometimes the gulfs between professional and amateur equipment, the new technologies that revolutionised design, and the often impractical ideas that bloomed briefly before falling by the wayside all contribute to the fascinating history of an invention that led to a popular hobby for many and a major industry that has touched us all.

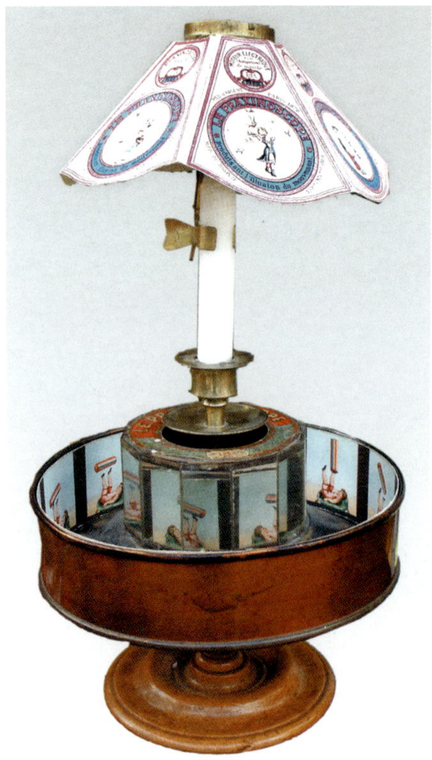

The Praxinoscope, a persistence of vision device from the 1870s, worked by placing a series of images on the inside of a revolving drum, viewed via a twelve-sided mirror at its centre. The images were illuminated by the light of a candle, positioned beneath a shaded area.

Early pioneers

What is believed to be the world's first still photograph was taken in 1826, using an impractical process and an eight-hour exposure. In 1839, with the announcement of the daguerreotype process, exposure times were reduced to minutes, with the image recorded on silver-plated copper. In 1841 the calotype process introduced paper negatives, and in 1850 images began to be made on glass plates, with exposure times at last reduced to fractions of a second.

Some enterprising pioneers, notably the British photographer Eadweard Muybridge, who was investigating animal movement at the time, produced moving images to be viewed in devices such as the Zoetrope using a series of still photographs taken on plates. But it was only with the advent of flexible film, rather than rigid plates, that it became possible to manufacture a true cine camera.

In 1885 George Eastman introduced the Eastman-Walker roller slide, incorporating a roll of paper film that fitted to the back of a still photography plate camera. Inventors such as Louis Le Prince immediately proposed the use of this paper film in an

Before cine cameras, simple moving images were sometimes produced by mechanical lantern slides. Essentially these were still images, made on glass and projected in a magic lantern, with elementary animation added mechanically to part of the image. In this example, a mouse appears to run into the mouth of a sleeping man.

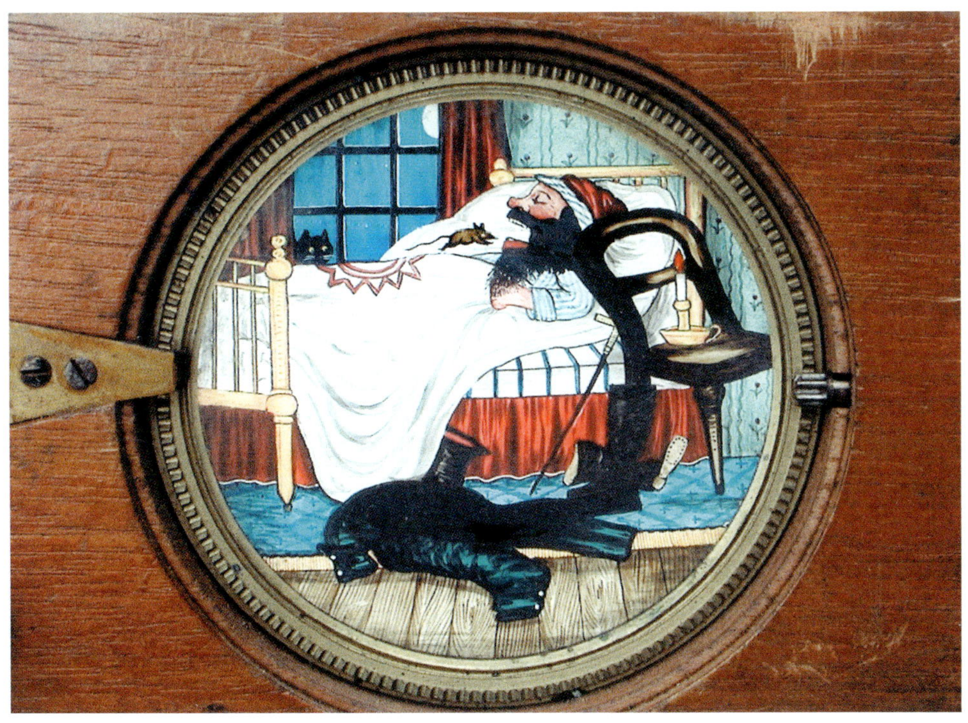

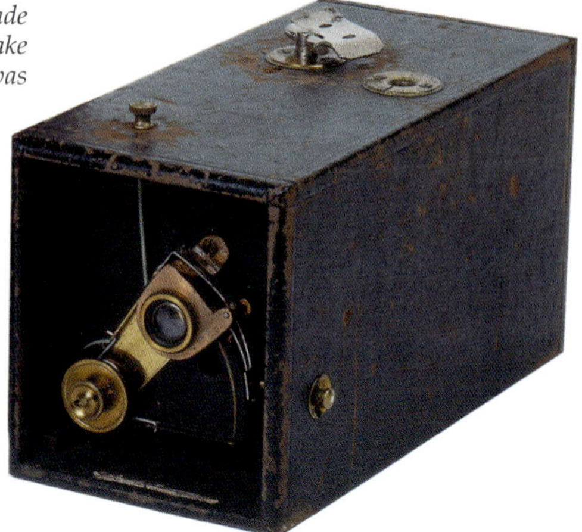

The Kodak was a still photography camera first made in 1888, and a subsequent model was the first to take flexible rollfilm with a celluloid base. The film was soon adopted by cine camera pioneers.

early incarnation of the cine camera. But the big turning point came in 1888, when Eastman introduced a camera known as the Kodak. It used paper film but was soon followed by a new model that used a different type of film based on transparent celluloid.

In the years that followed, many inventors began looking seriously at how this new celluloid film might be introduced into a moving picture camera. Among them was William Friese-Green, a major English pioneer who had already experimented with strips of paper soaked in castor oil to make them transparent. In 1890 he was among the first to demonstrate moving pictures, recorded on celluloid film and projected on to a screen. When he died in 1921 his tombstone claimed him to have been the inventor of commercial kinematography.

In fact many pioneers had worked on the same idea, but the man who brought moving pictures to the attention of the public was the American Thomas Edison, inventor of, among other things, the phonograph. It was actually his assistant William Dickson who suggested using celluloid film, and in 1893 Edison announced two pieces of equipment: the Kinetograph, which exposed the necessary sequence of pictures on 35 mm wide film, and the Kinetoscope, a special viewer that allowed only one person at a time to see the picture sequence as a moving image.

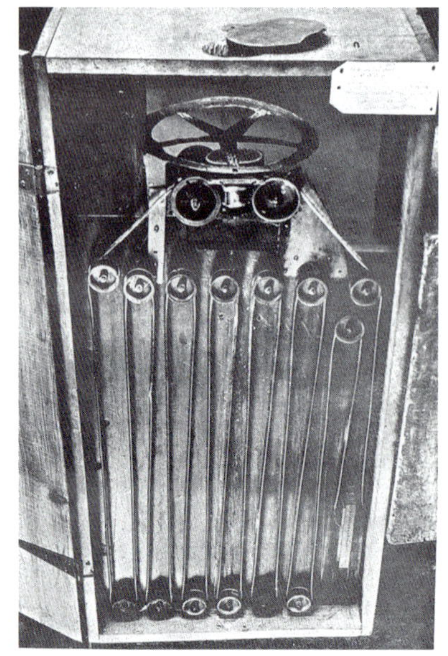

Thomas Edison's Kinetoscope showed moving images in 1893, but they could be viewed by only one person at a time.

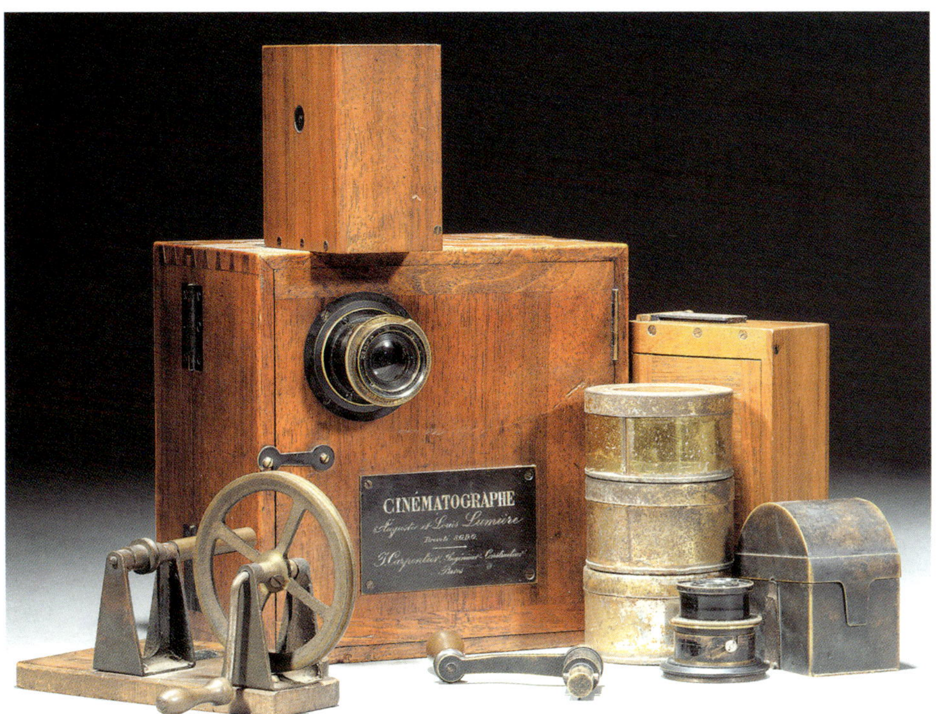

Edison's equipment was installed in kinetoscope and phonograph parlours across the United States. In London, kinetoscopes were found in converted shops, where viewing cost tuppence (two pennies in that era's pre-decimal currency) per person.

The kinetoscope was successful, but restrictive. What was needed next was a device that would project the moving image on to a screen for a larger audience. Once again, there are numerous claims from different inventors about who got there first, but the French brothers Auguste and Louis Lumière are the ones who are most usually credited with the achievement, with their introduction of the Cinematographe, a combined camera, projector and printer. It was demonstrated in public for the first time in 1895.

Meanwhile, in England, Birt Acres, the newly appointed general manager of Elliott & Son, a photographic plate company, was already becoming enthusiastic about moving pictures. His invention, the Kinetic Camera, exposed a long series of images on a strip of 70 mm wide celluloid film. Using this method, Acres attempted to film the opening of the Manchester Ship Canal in January 1894. His effort was unsuccessful, although he did manage to obtain images of that year's Henley Regatta.

The Cinematographe was designed by the French brothers Auguste and Louis Lumière and was made by Jules Carpentier of Paris in 1895. It was the first viable movie projector and doubled as a camera. It is seen here with accessories that include a supplementary Ross lens and a rare Lumière film winder.

A year later Acres patented a rather more practical device, called the Kineopticon, which used 35 mm wide film, and he went on to become probably the first newsreel photographer. He made 35 mm films of the English University Boat Race and the Derby in 1895 and was invited to Germany to film the celebrations that marked the opening of the Kiel Canal.

All this was achieved with cameras that were difficult and clumsy to operate, relying on a handle on the camera's side to wind the film through the body and needing a tripod to support them during filming. Camera operators of the time developed the knack of keeping the handle cranked at a steady rate in order that the projected film would not show the action speeding up and slowing down unnecessarily.

Movie equipment of this era could be divided broadly into two classes. In the first, an intermittently turning sprocket wheel, interacting with sprocket holes in the film, pulled the film through a gate in the camera body in a series of stop-start jerks. In the second, part of the film hung in a loose loop, with the intermittent stop-start motion applied by a claw mechanism to sprocket holes in the film only within that loop, while the rest of the machinery ran smoothly and continuously. In each method, various forms of shutter allowed light to pass through the lens and on to the film for only the split second that it was stationary in the gate. Although the first process was the most obvious one for early pioneers, it was the latter that won the day and became the norm.

The names briefly mentioned here are of those who have gone down in history as being significant pioneers in the development of early cine cameras, but they were by no means alone. As the twentieth century dawned, a multitude of inventors in England, France, Germany and the United States all tried, tested and demonstrated different ways to achieve a similar end. And with every new approach, very often came a new gauge – the actual width of the film – and positioning of the sprocket holes in the film that facilitated its movement through the camera.

Gauges that were tried with various degrees of success included 13 mm, 15 mm, 17.5 mm, 21 mm, 28 mm, 38 mm, 50 mm, 54 mm, 60 mm and 63 mm. But the gauge that eventually became the standard was 35 mm, derived from taking the

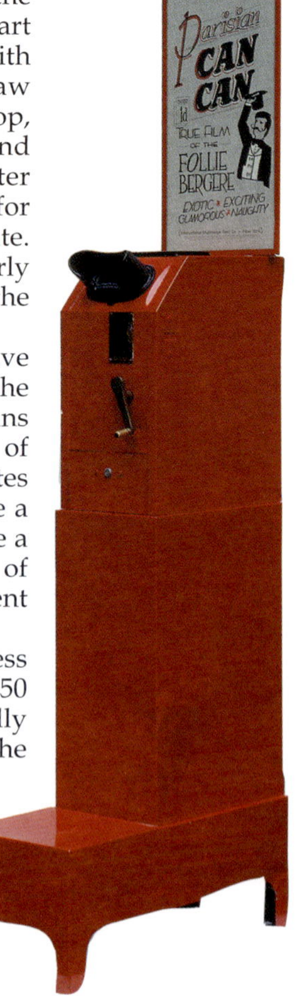

The Mutoscope, introduced in 1897, showed a series of still images shot on a Biograph camera, which used 65 mm wide film, wound past the lens with intermittent stops for each exposure. The resulting pictures were attached by one edge to a drum inside the Mutoscope that revolved as the viewer turned a handle.

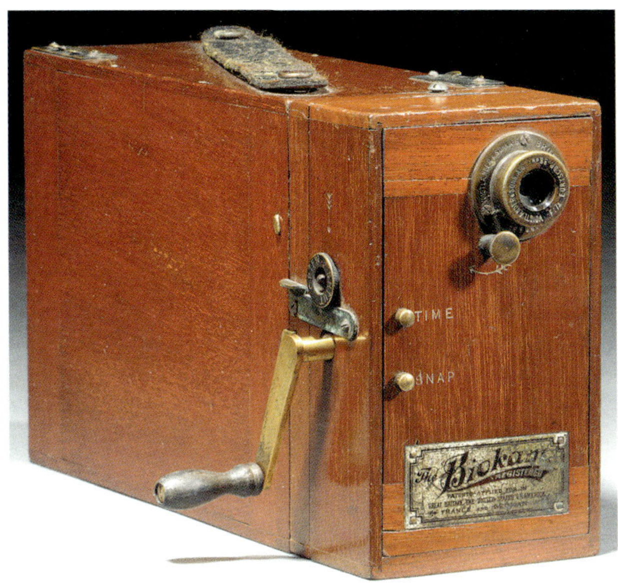

The Biokam, introduced in 1899, was made by Alfred Darling. It took 17.5 mm film and, as well as shooting moving images, could be adjusted to take still-photography snapshots and time exposures.

70 mm wide film used by Eastman in his Kodak still photography camera and simply cutting it in half.

As a result of all this experimentation it was not long before a new silent-film industry emerged. The first building to be

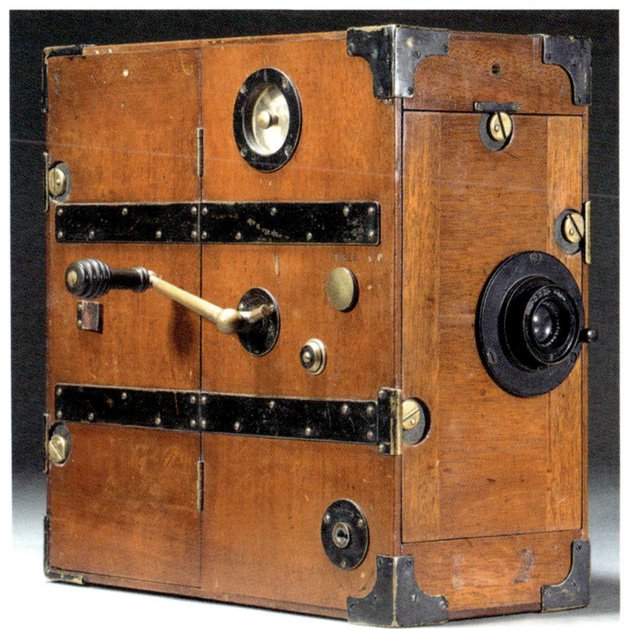

The Cinematographic Camera, made by Alfred Darling around 1900, was a hand-cranked model made to use 35 mm film.

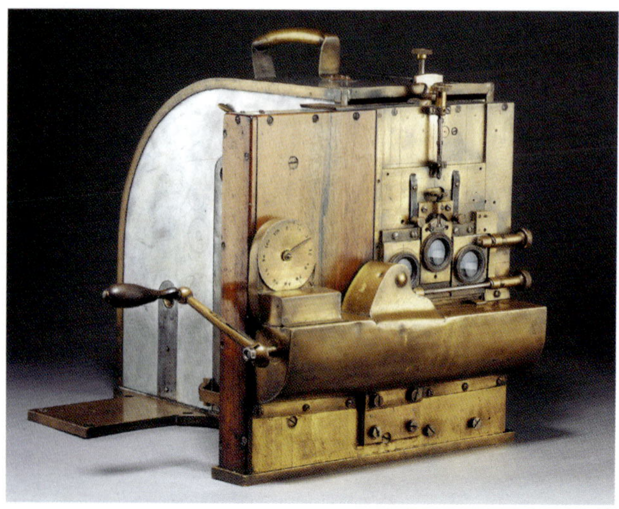

constructed for the purpose was Edison's Black Maria studio, so called because subjects stood against a black background to produce the most sharply defined pictures. The studio, built in 1893, could be rotated so that its stage caught the sun all day.

Shot on location in 1897, the Corbett-Fitzsimmons fight at Carson City, Nevada, was shown to an audience on a film 11,000 feet (3353 metres) in length. But it was not until 1903 that a film

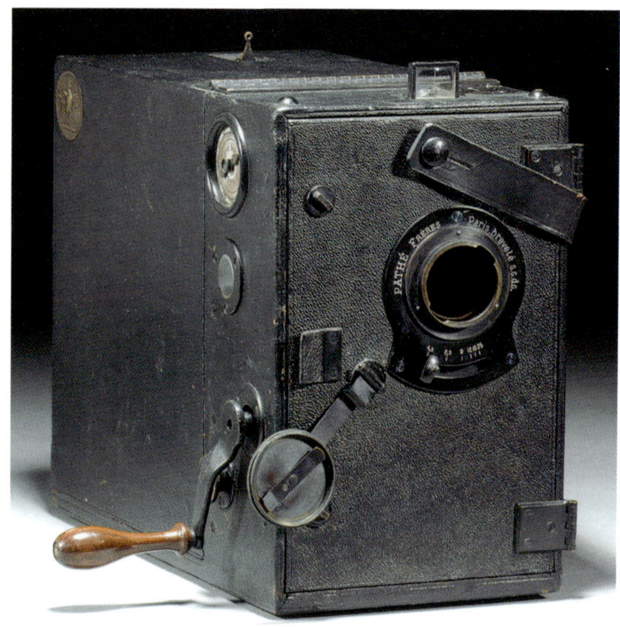

The Aeroscope, made in 1920 by the British firm Eracam, was a 35 mm camera that was unusual in having a motor driven by compressed air, charged by a foot pump or pocket-sized cylinders. Made to be used without a tripod, this camera was attached to the operator by a belt and shoulder sling.

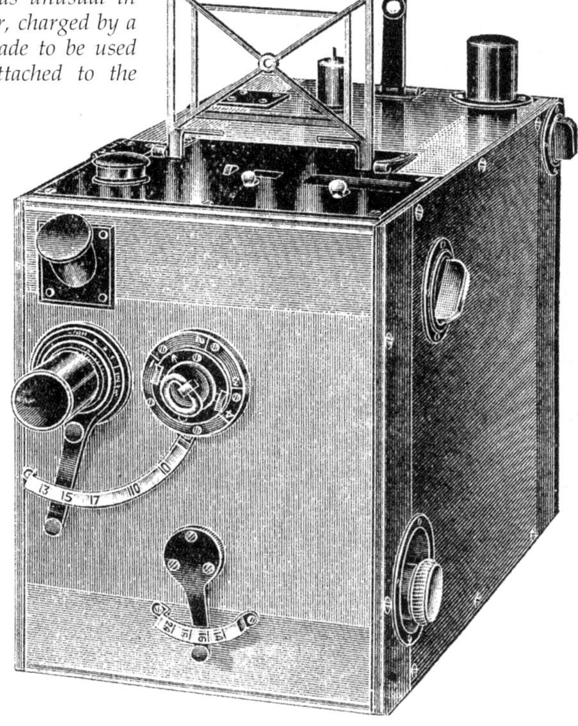

maker, Edwin S. Porter, attempted to use the new medium to produce a fictional film – *The Great Train Robbery*.

Cameras in these early years were used primarily by professional film makers or sometimes expedition photographers, with amateur photographers excluded by the price of buying and running the equipment. That situation, however, was about to change.

The advent of amateur cine

In the late nineteenth and early twentieth centuries amateur photography was a popular hobby; but making the move from still to cine photography was prohibitively expensive for the average amateur. So it was that camera manufacturers sought ways to reduce costs and bring cine to the man in the street.

The first to produce a camera aimed squarely at the amateur market was Birt Acres, who in 1898 patented the Birtac Home Cinema designed, in the words of the camera's handbook, 'to place animated photography within the reach of everyone'. It was a camera and projector combined, which economised on film by splitting 35 mm down the centre and coming up with the 17.5 mm gauge.

The same gauge was used the following year by Alfred Darling, manufacturer of the wood and brass Biokam camera, which could be used for both movie and still pictures. Another year later the Gaumont company in France introduced the Chrono de Poche, which used 15 mm film.

These and many more cameras were made with the aim of reducing costs by using narrower film gauges. In the end, however, it was the professional movie world that really kick-started amateur cine enthusiasm, not for cameras *per se*, but for their use with projectors.

There was at this time a growing interest in the commercial cinema and, as domestic electricity began to take over from gas, enthusiasts bought small projectors for home use, showing cut-down versions of commercial silent films of the day. The 28 mm

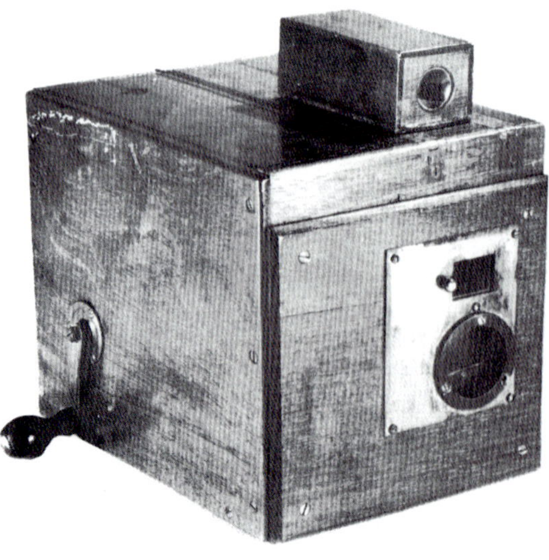

The Birtac is acknowledged as the first cine camera to have been aimed at amateurs. Invented by Birt Acres as part of a complete home cinema system, it economised on film by using a new 17.5 mm gauge. The same equipment was used for projecting the film.

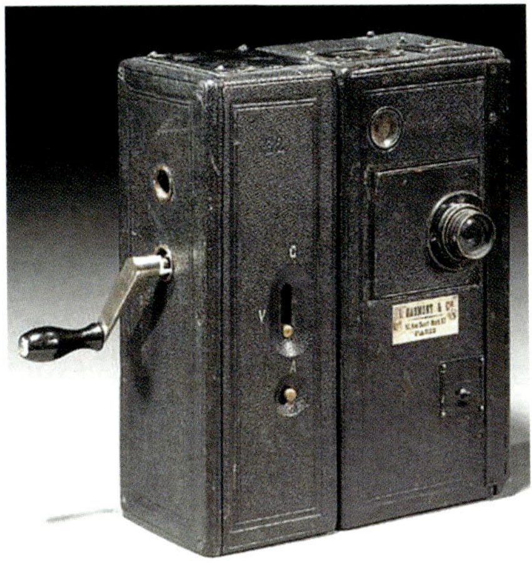

In 1900 the Chrono de Poche, made by Gaumont in France, used 15 mm film with the sprocket holes in the centre. The camera was a commercialised version of the Chronophotographe d'Amateur, devised by George Demeny in 1893 to shoot picture sequences for viewing on a picture disc machine.

gauge, introduced by Pathé in a 1912 projector called the Pathé Kok, was a particular favourite and this new gauge remained popular for some years.

True amateur cinematography began, however, in 1922, when Pathé introduced the Baby projector, again designed to show cut-down versions of commercial cinema films and newsreels, this time with a new 9.5 mm gauge. The following year the same company launched the Pathé Baby camera, which, for the first time, was capable of shooting 9.5 mm film. The same year, in the United States, the Eastman Company launched the Cine Kodak,

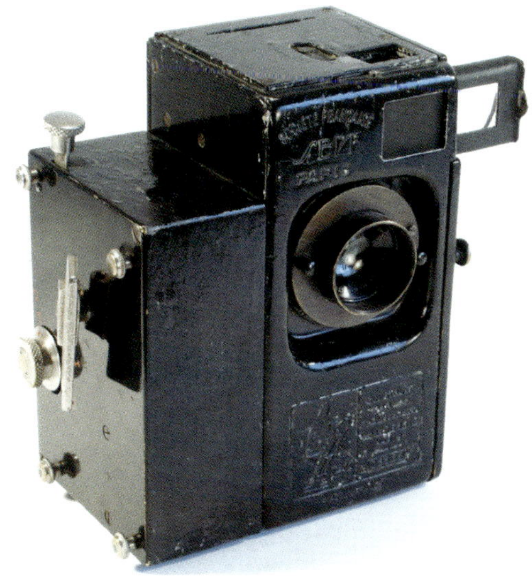

The Debrie Photo-Cine Sept, launched in 1922, took 35 mm film for hand-held short runs of movie action but was also known as a 35 mm still camera with a built-in clockwork motor drive.

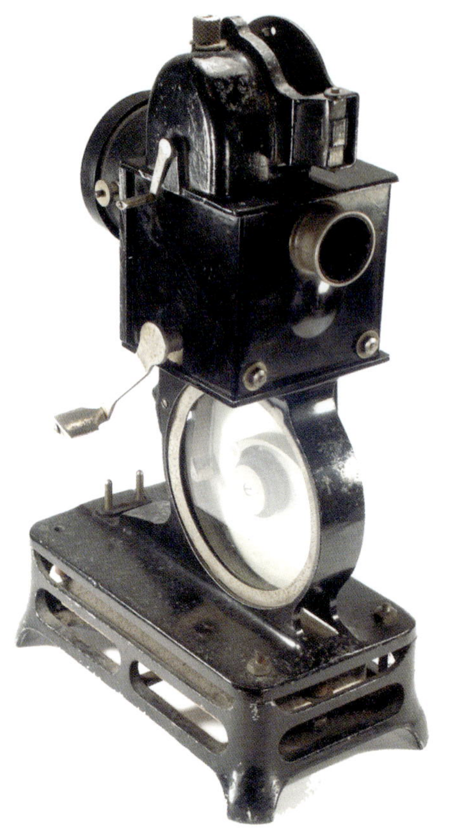

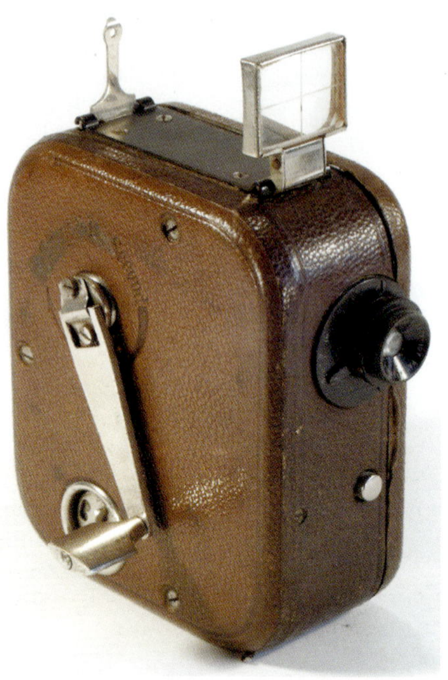

Above: *The hand-cranked Pathé Baby cine camera, launched in 1923 as a companion to the Baby projector, was operated with two turns of the handle per second. It was the first cine camera to shoot 9.5 mm film.*

Above left: *The Pathé Baby, which first appeared in 1922, was a projector made to show cut-down versions of the day's silent cinema successes, printed for the purpose on 9.5 mm film.*

Left: *The Cine-Kodak, launched in 1923, introduced the new 16 mm gauge. This hand-cranked camera was box-shaped, with the main controls on the back of the body. An eye-level viewfinder, which passed through the body, could be changed to accommodate waist-level use.*

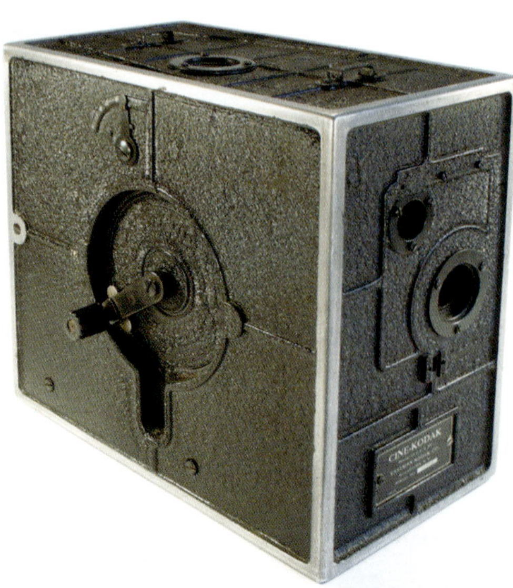

the first cine camera to take 16 mm film. Together, these two cameras revolutionised amateur cinematography.

The advent of 16 mm film with smaller images made a significant saving by offering a running time two and a half times that of an equivalent length of 35 mm film. A second saving came from the way the film was processed – not as a negative, which then had to be turned into a positive print, as was previously the case, but as a positive image. Total savings over using the more conventional 35 mm film came out at around 80 per cent.

The 9.5 mm film used by Pathé, despite being narrower than 16 mm, gave only a slightly smaller image size, of 8.3 x 6.5 mm rather than 9.65 x 7.21 mm, which was achieved by placing the sprocket holes in the centre, between the frames, as opposed to the sides, which naturally reduced the space available for the actual image.

With the advent of these two new gauges many of the other odd sizes rapidly died away, leaving three basic camera types: 35 mm, known then as the standard gauge, for professionals; and 16 mm and 9.5 mm, known as sub-standard gauges, for amateurs. Innovations and new camera designs soon began to flow thick and fast.

The first manufacturer to follow Kodak's lead with a 16 mm camera was the American Bell & Howell company in 1925. Its Filmo 70 was a highly stylised, oval-shaped camera with the lens

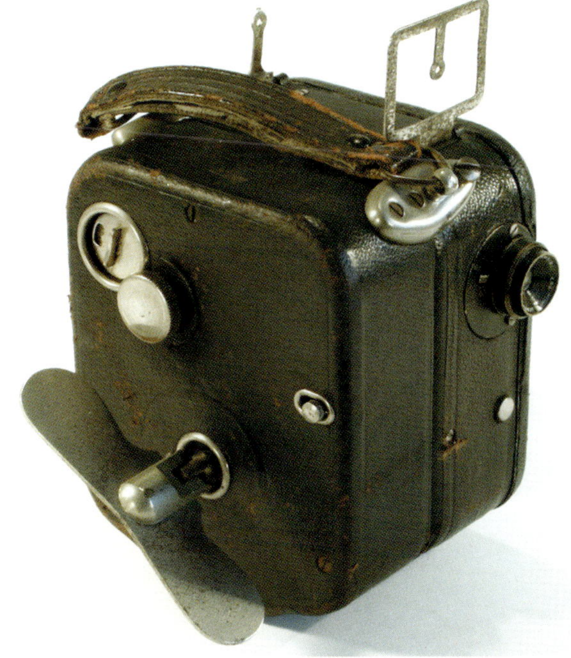

In 1926 the Pathé Baby camera became easier to use, because of the addition of two add-on clockwork motors. Seen here is the camera with its Motrix attachment. The other was the Cameo, which allowed more filming per wind.

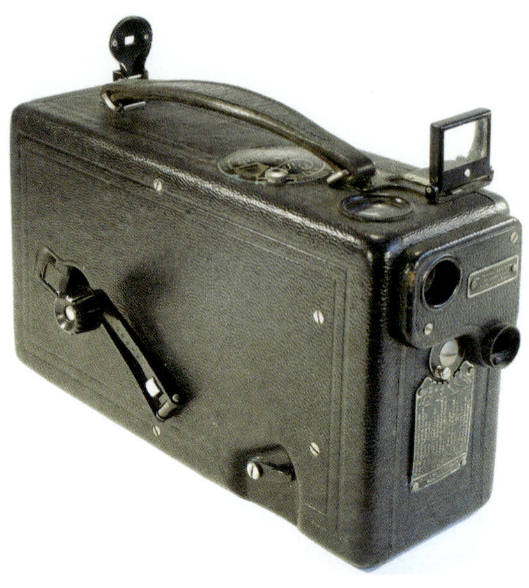

Launched in 1926, the new Cine-Kodak Model B was a much slimmer camera than the original model, economising on space by means of the film spools being arranged one on top of the other instead of side by side. It took 50 foot or 100 foot (15 or 30 metre) spools of film and was driven by clockwork.

and shutter mechanism attached to a square mount to the side and front. Unlike the hand-cranked Kodak, it utilised a clockwork motor, making it far better suited to hand-held filming.

Kodak's answer came the following year with a clockwork-driven restyling of its original camera. It called the new version the Cine-Kodak Model B, and only then did the first camera become known as the Model A. The new camera took 16 mm film in lengths of 50 or 100 feet (approximately 15 or 30 metres). It attained its new trim shape by positioning the spools on top of each other, separated by a hinged flap, rather than in the conventional positions top and bottom of the body.

The next innovation was the three-lens turret. The standard lens sold with most cameras gave a view approximate to that seen by the human eye, whereas a telephoto lens could bring distant subjects closer, and a wide-angle lens would open up the scene to allow more subject matter at the sides, top and bottom. Lenses of this type were already available for interchanging with the standard, but the new idea of mounting all three on a rotating turret, turned to bring any one of them into play in an instant, brought a new versatility to amateur film making.

The American Victor Animatograph Company claimed, in its advertisements, to be the first to offer such a feature, with its Model 3-T, launched in

The body styling of the Ensign Auto Kinecam in 1928 was very reminiscent of that of the Bell & Howell cameras of a few years before, and a similar style was to be seen from many other manufacturers of 16 mm equipment in the coming years.

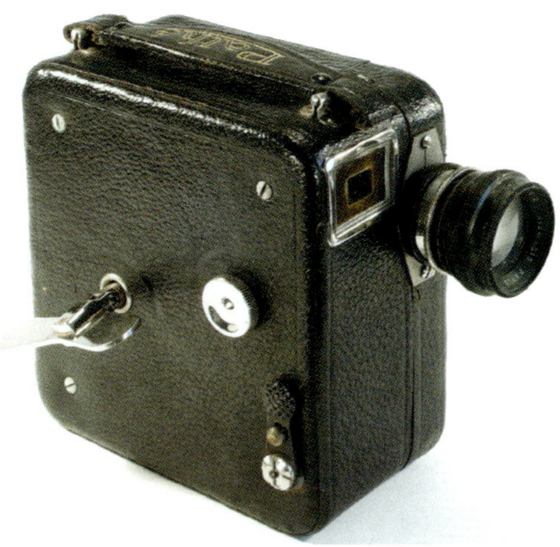

The Pathé Motocamera, which appeared in 1928, was made for 9.5 mm film and used a clockwork motor that drove the whole 30 feet (9 metres) at a single winding. The camera was used by an English company called A. O. Roth as the basis for several customised versions of its own.

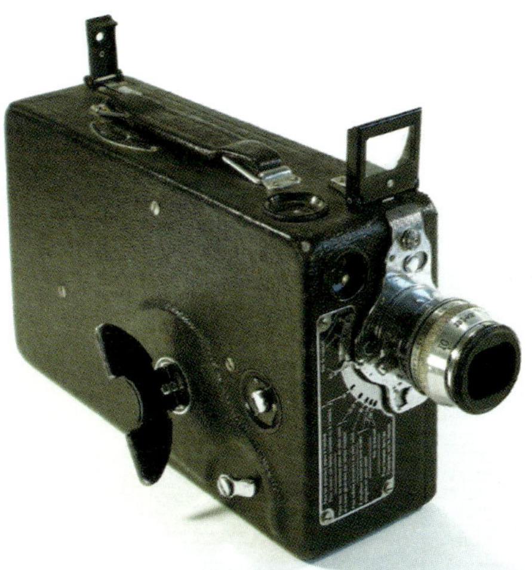

Right: *The Cine-Kodak Model BB, made in 1929, had a more streamlined and smaller body than the Model B but took only 50 foot (15 metre) film spools. Pushing a button in the side instantly halved the shooting speed.*

1928, although Bell & Howell may actually have been the first with the Filmo 70C, launched around the same time, which also sported the three-lens turret.

Although many of these cameras were still large and unwieldy unless used on a tripod, some manufacturers of the era attempted to make equipment smaller than ever before. The Kinamo camera, made first by Ica in 1924 and then by Zeiss Ikon in 1929, measured a mere 10 x 8.5 x 5.5 cm (3.9 x 3.3 x 2.2 inches), despite taking a full-size 16 mm image.

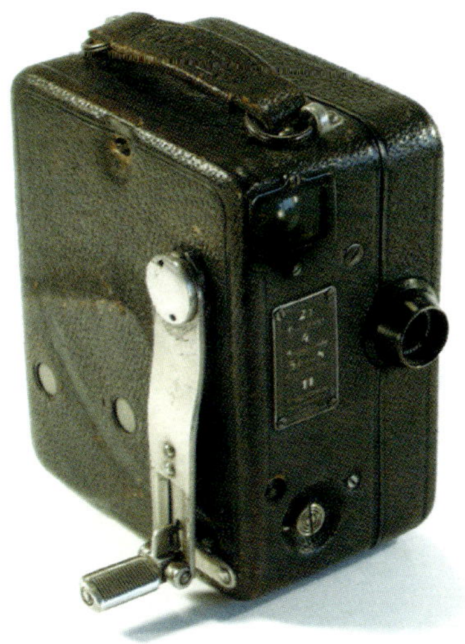

The Kinamo S10, made by Zeiss Ikon in 1929, was one of the smallest of all 16 mm cameras, using daylight-loading cartridges, each containing 32 feet (about 10 metres) of film. Clockwork-driven, it was unusual for having an indicator to record the state of spring tension.

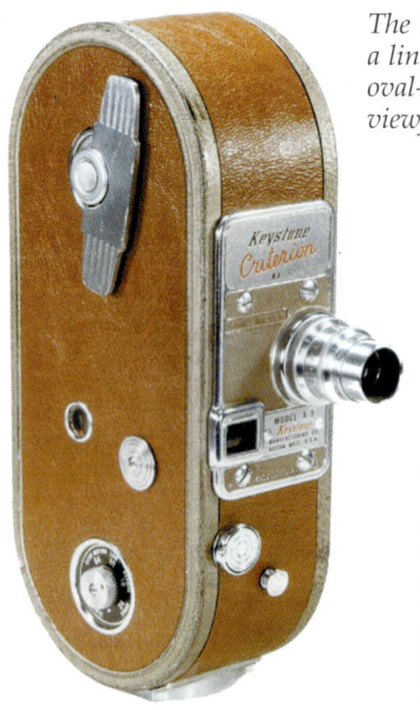

The 16 mm Keystone Criterion Model A, made in 1930, was the first in a line of cameras from the company to adopt a slightly unconventional, oval-shaped body. It was also unusual in its positioning of the viewfinder below the level of the lens.

Below: Within only a few years of the introduction of amateur cine cameras, the new hobby began to be illustrated on postcards of the time. This one, postmarked 1931, shows an artist's impression that was clearly influenced by the first Cine-Kodak.

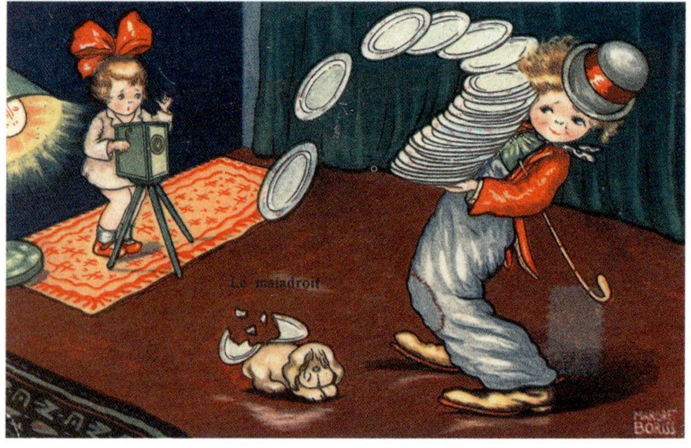

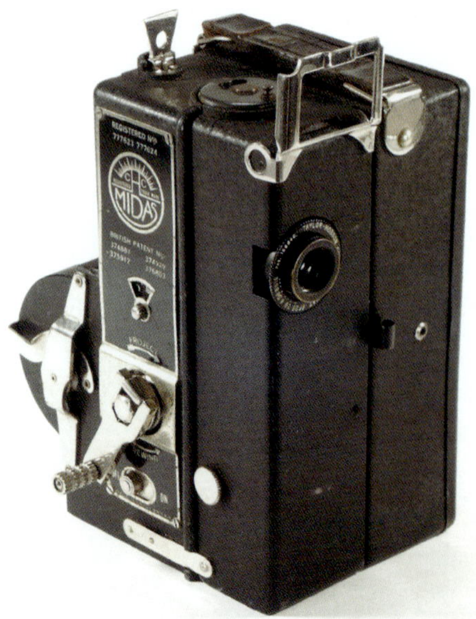

Left: The Midas, made in 1933, used 9.5 mm film, with a battery-driven motor when filming. The camera could also be used as a projector, when the same batteries lit a torch bulb inside the body. To conserve power, film transport when projecting was operated by a handle.

Around the same time there came a short resurrection of a style that went back to the start of cine-camera manufacture: that of combining a camera with a projector. The London-based Home Cine Cameras Limited tried the idea in 1927 with a series of 35 mm Campro models, then again in 1935 with a 9.5 mm version. Camera-Projector Limited, another London company, also made a 9.5 mm camera cum projector, called the Midas, in 1933. Both used the same mechanism for shooting and projecting, and incorporated torch bulbs into their bodies for the latter purpose.

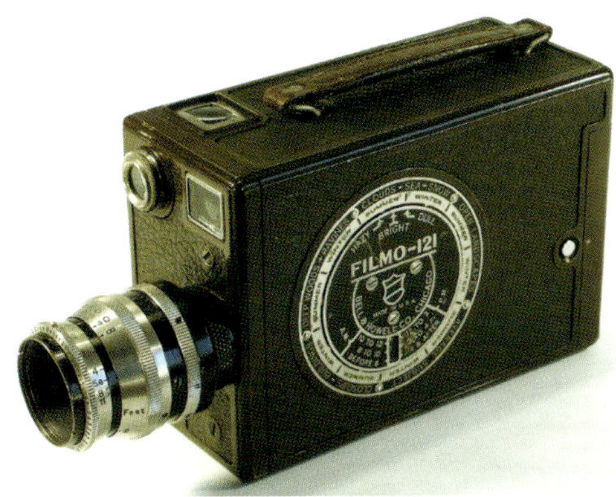

In 1934 the Bell & Howell Filmo 21 was a small, compact 16 mm film cartridge camera with a waist-level as well as an eye-level viewfinder. When the clockwork drive ran down, the motor stopped dead, rather than slowing gradually, as was the case with many cameras of this era.

Although having an Art Deco design, the Dekko camera took its name from the Hindi word for 'look'. This model, made of Bakelite, took 9.5 mm film and first appeared in 1934.

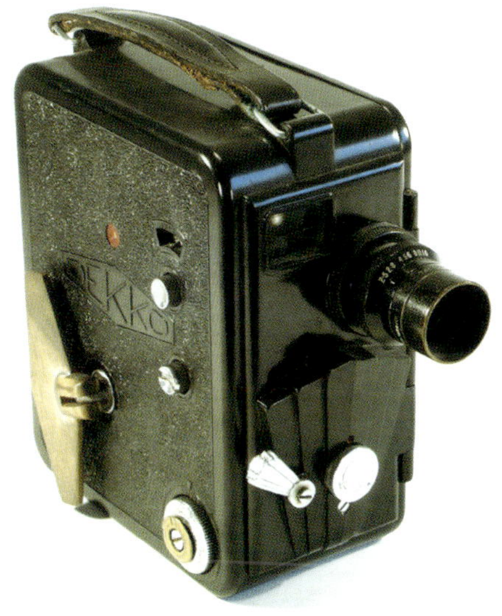

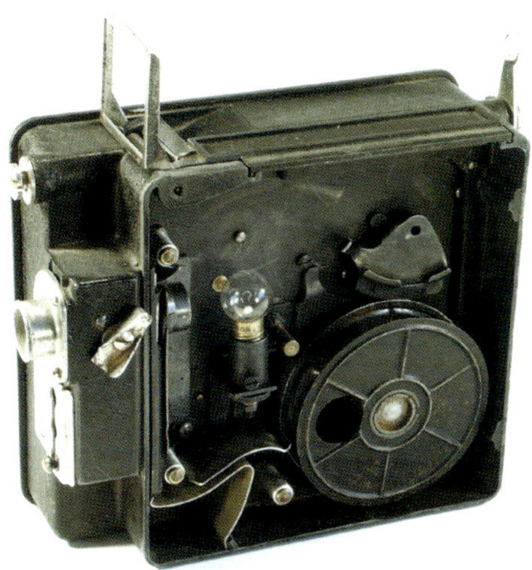

Campro cameras could also be used as projectors with a suitable battery or transformer plugged into the side to illuminate a torch bulb inside the body. Film transport was clockwork-driven for both shooting and projecting. This 9.5 mm model was made in 1935.

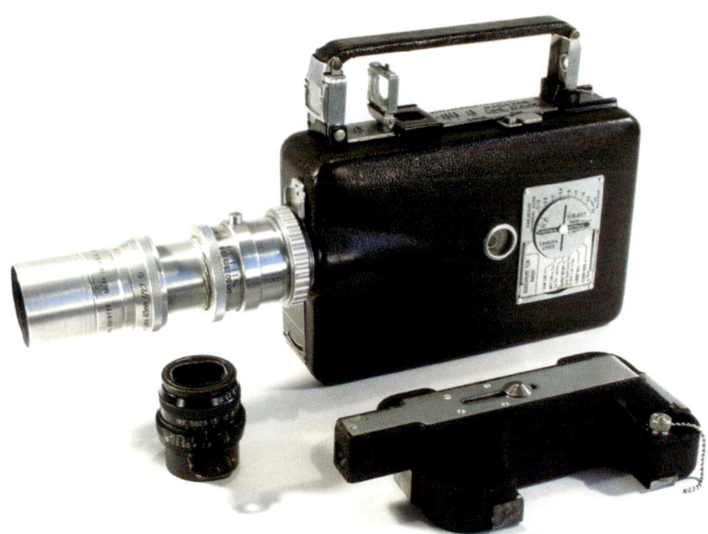

Made in 1936, the Magazine Cine-Kodak took 16 mm film in a cartridge, which could be interchanged with an unusual reflex focusing accessory that allowed accurate focusing before, but not during, shooting.

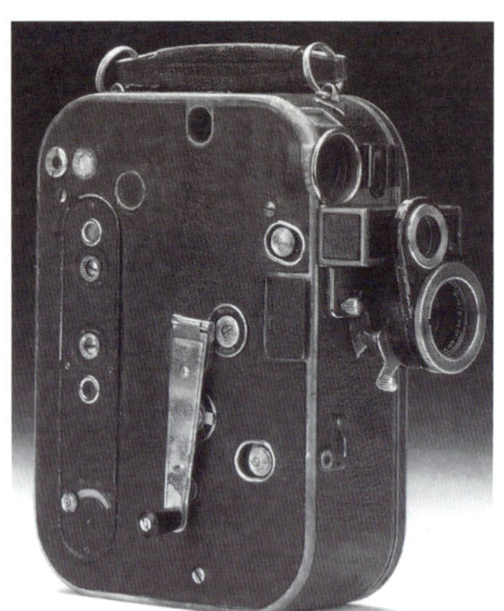

Left: The Movikon 16, made by Zeiss Ikon in 1936, was a compact 16 mm camera with eye-level and waist-level viewfinders and interchangeable lenses. A small number of these cameras were supplied to the German Air Force.

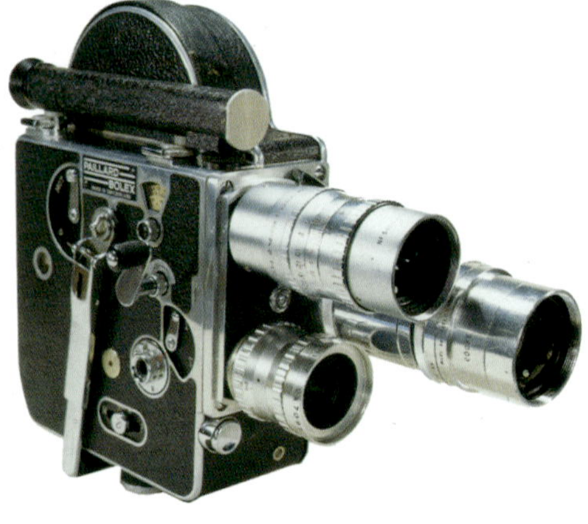

In 1936 the Swiss Paillard company introduced the H16, the first in a range of highly sophisticated 16 mm Bolex cameras that, in the years to come, would be taken up more by professionals than by amateur film makers. This one is the Series IV, which was launched in 1947. The H8, a similar design but made for 8 mm film, was introduced in 1938.

The electrically driven Cine Camera Gun, manufactured by the British Williamson Manufacturing Company in 1937, was designed to train Royal Air Force observers and pilots in aerial gunnery.

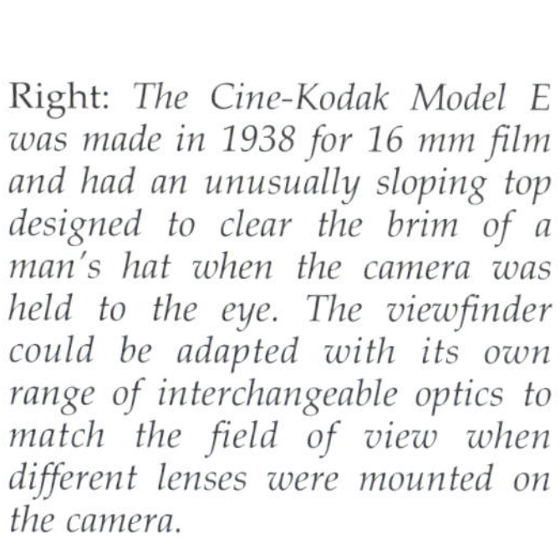

Right: The Cine-Kodak Model E was made in 1938 for 16 mm film and had an unusually sloping top designed to clear the brim of a man's hat when the camera was held to the eye. The viewfinder could be adapted with its own range of interchangeable optics to match the field of view when different lenses were mounted on the camera.

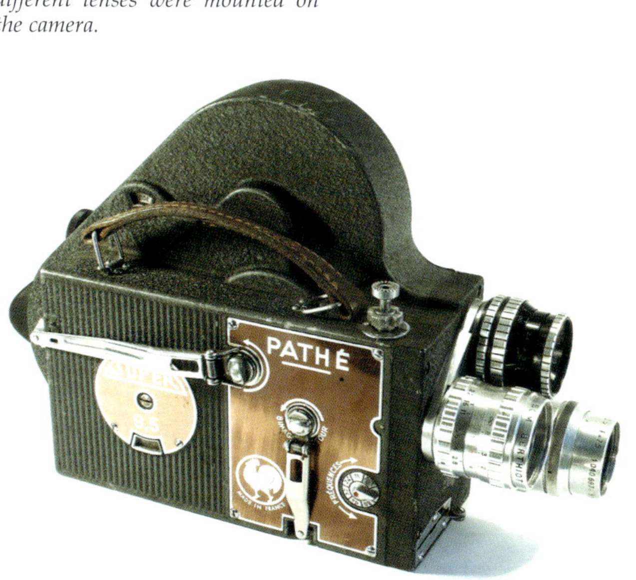

The Pathé Webo Super, available in 9.5 mm and 16 mm versions, appealed to serious amateurs and professionals alike. The cameras, launched in the mid 1950s, featured three-lens turrets and were among the earliest cameras to include a reflex viewfinder, which looked through the lens, alongside the more traditional optical finder.

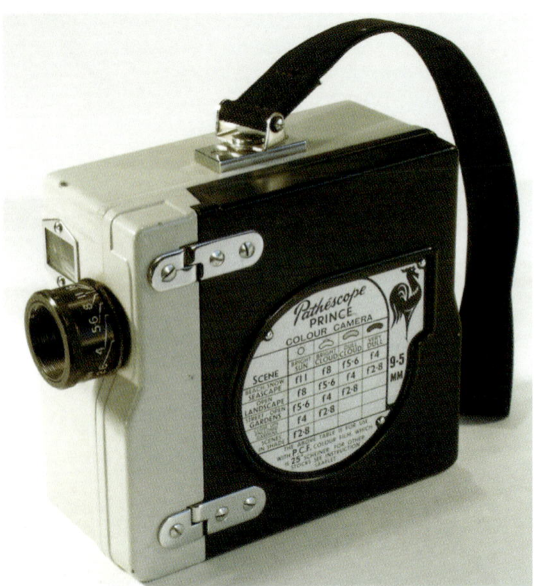

Even as late as 1959 the Pathescope company was still pushing the 9.5 mm gauge. This is the Prince, which doubled as a still-photography snapshot camera, taking one frame at a time.

With cameras getting smaller, easier and more convenient to use, it seemed that amateur cinematography was now well established in both the 16 mm and the 9.5 mm gauges. But in 1932 Kodak once again changed everything with the introduction of the 8 mm gauge. Although 16 mm and 9.5 mm still remained popular among amateur movie makers for many years more, 8 mm soon proved itself to be the most popular amateur film gauge of all time.

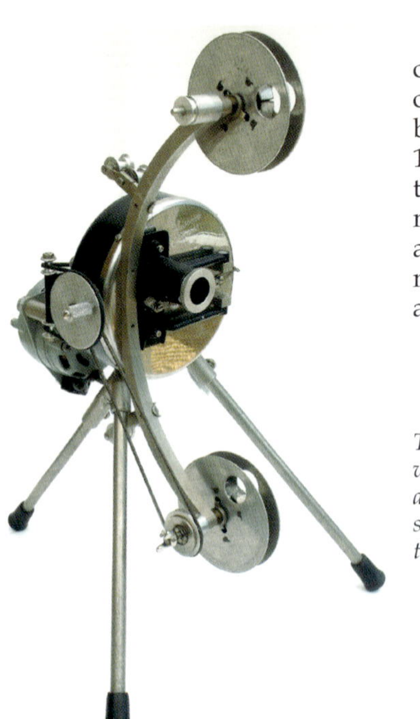

The Pathescope Princess was a special projector made for use with the Prince camera. A motor drove the film for movies, but a manual handle could also be employed to wind through single frames, taken in the Prince's snapshot mode, one at a time.

The 8 mm boom years

Back in 1914 Kodak had experimented briefly with a cine camera that shot two images side by side on 35 mm film. In 1932 the company updated that idea and introduced a new camera that shot two images side by side on special 25 foot (7.6 metre) lengths of 16 mm film that used twice the usual number of sprocket holes on each side. To get the two images side by side, the film was run through the camera once, removed, turned over and run back again on to its original spool. After processing, the film was split down the middle and the two ends joined to make one 50 foot (15 metre) length of film for projection, with a single set of sprocket holes down one side. Known first as 'Double-8', the new gauge soon became referred to as 'Standard-8'.

The first camera to use Standard-8 was the Cine-Kodak Eight-20, a slim, clockwork-driven model with its viewfinder built into the carrying handle. Inside, it deviated from what would eventually become the more conventional approach to design in which film would be fed past the shutter by two sprocket wheels at the top and bottom of the gate. The Kodak camera, rather, used one large sprocket wheel behind the lens both to feed the film into the gate and to take it up again on the

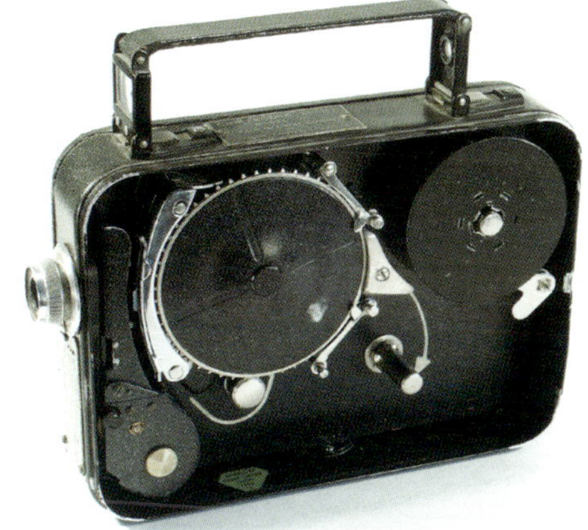

The first Standard-8 camera was the Cine-Kodak Eight-20, launched in 1932 along with a new black-and-white film that was processed – like 16 mm before it – as a direct positive to maintain low-cost shooting.

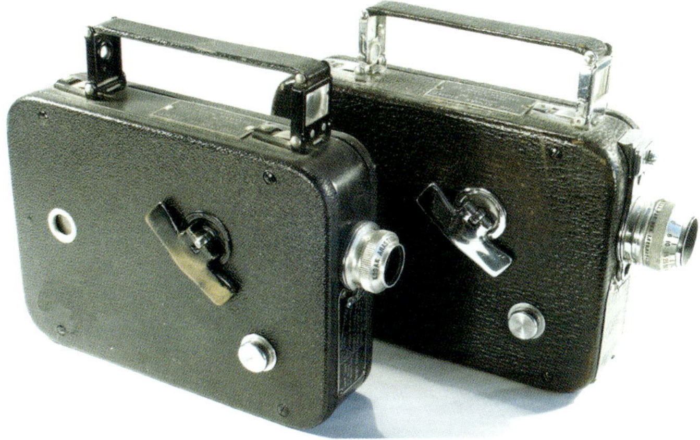

Kodak's Eight-20 camera was followed in 1933 by the Eight-25, which had a slightly better lens, and the Eight-60, which offered interchangeable lenses and a viewfinder that could be adapted to suit whichever lens was on the camera at the time.

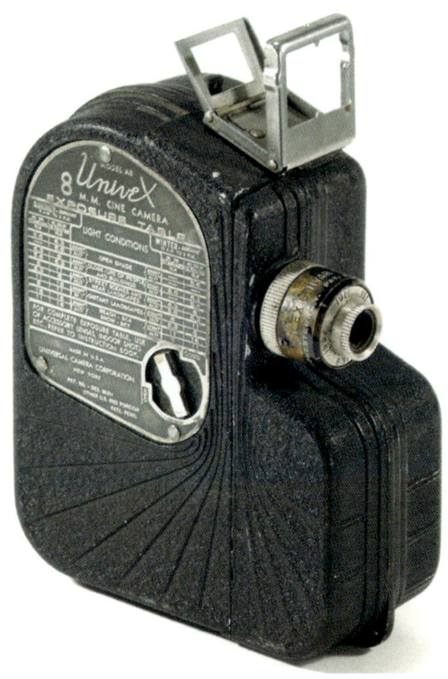

In 1936 the Universal Camera Corporation introduced a rival 8 mm system, which it called Single-8. The Univex A-8 was the camera that pioneered the 8 mm gauge, which, after an initial degree of success, fell by the wayside.

other side, a style influenced by some 16 mm cameras of the day.

Soon after Kodak's launch, its dominance in the market-place was challenged by the American Universal Camera Corporation, which was known for introducing inexpensive still cameras to the masses using its own unique film sizes. Following that logic, the company introduced the Univex A-8 cine camera, which sold in 1936 for $9.95, using Universal's own patented 30 foot (9 metre) spools of film, 8 mm in width and designed to be run through the camera only once.

Universal called its new gauge 'Single-8' and sold 250,000 cameras in two years. A few other manufacturers, notably Bell & Howell and Agfa, followed with their own Single-8 cameras, while Universal continued with further new models of its own, but in the end it was Kodak that won the battle.

Although there had been proposals for shooting in colour as far back as 1901, films of this era were generally still black and white. Kodak had introduced Kodacolor for still photography in 1913, and an experimental movie version appeared in 1915. But it was not until 1936 that a much-improved colour film,

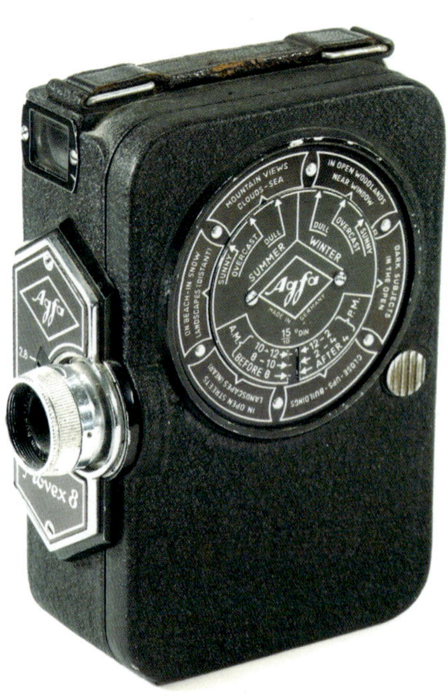

Agfa was one of the few companies to follow the Single-8 route. Its Movex 8, launched in 1937, differed from the Univex, however, by incorporating the film in an easy-load, drop-in cartridge.

using a different technology and now called 'Kodachrome', became available for 8 mm gauge movie makers. The film could be processed only by Kodak, and it was never made in a Single-8 version. So, as amateur cinematographers abandoned the old black-and-white film in favour of colour, they were forced to use Standard-8 cameras and the brief enthusiasm for Universal's Single-8 gauge quickly died.

Standard-8 won the day, but not always in the same form. Agfa and then Kodak introduced cameras that incorporated the film into a simple drop-in cartridge, rather than being on reels, to make loading easier. The idea was taken up for a while by other makers too, including Bell & Howell.

During the late 1930s and into the 1940s, not only the film but also the design of 8 mm cameras began to change quite radically. Keystone, for example, took its old 16 mm designs and simply scaled them down to 8 mm. Others went for entirely new styles, such as the Eumig Electric C4, made in 1938, which offered the first example of an electric motor in an 8 mm amateur cine

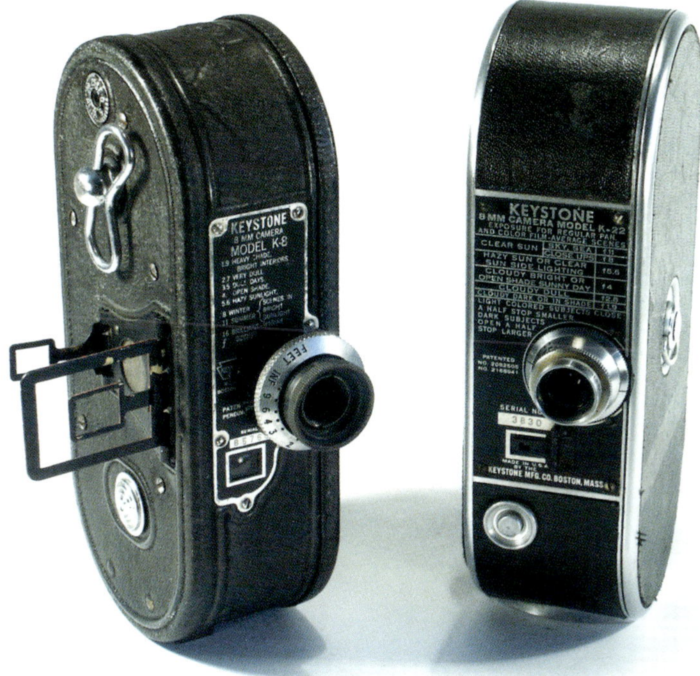

New designs of cine camera began to emerge in the 1930s. The American Keystone company took its 16 mm style, seen previously in the Criterion Model A, and scaled it down for 8 mm film, represented here by the K-8 and K-22, both made in 1936.

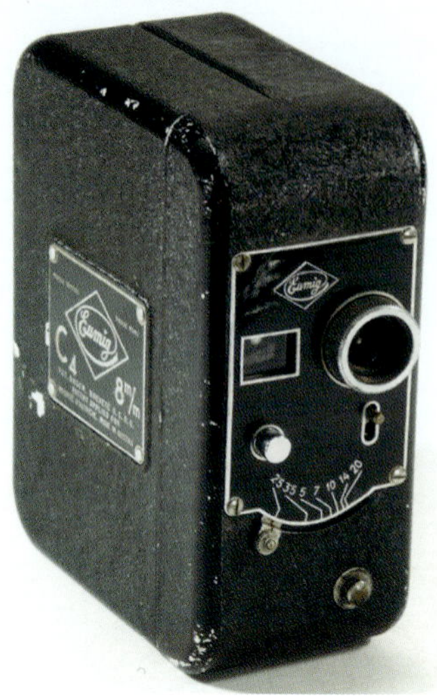

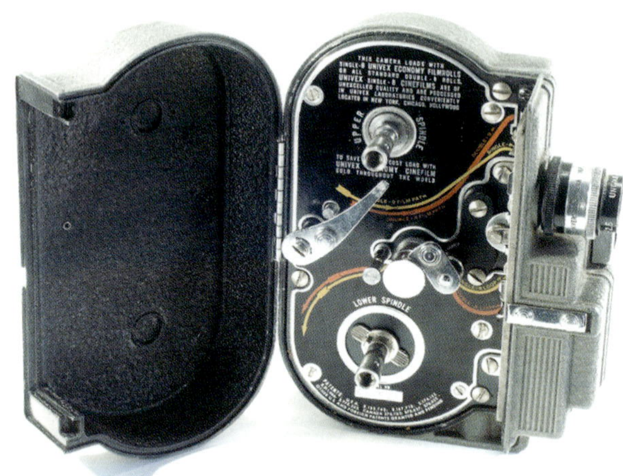

Left: *In 1938 Eumig introduced the Electric C-4, the first amateur cine camera to use an electric, rather than a clockwork, motor.*

Above: *When it became clear that Standard-8 would win the day, Universal began making cameras to take both Single-8 and Standard-8 film in the same body. This model is the Cinemaster G-8, made in 1941.*

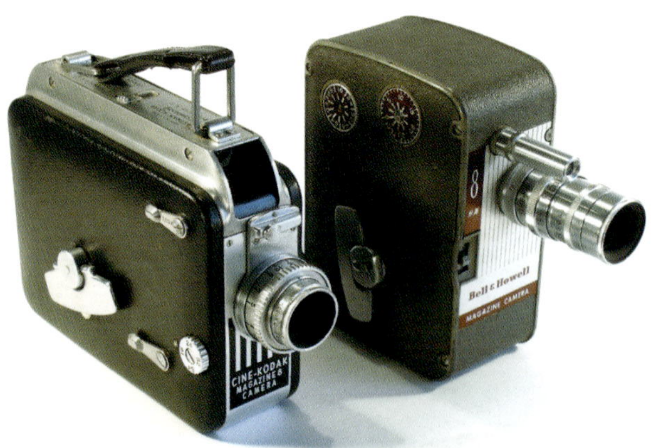

Left: *In the 1940s Standard-8 film, preloaded into cartridges, became popular for a while. Kodak used the style in its Cine-Kodak Magazine-8 camera, made in 1946, while Bell & Howell followed on in 1947 with the Magazine 172 camera.*

camera. In the same year came the introduction, by the Austrian company Ditmar, of the first 8 mm camera to incorporate a built-in exposure meter. This was an extinction meter that used a step wedge, showing six degrees of density, in the viewfinder. As the camera operator adjusted the aperture control on the side of the camera, a needle moved up and down this wedge, and when it fell against the last discernible portion, the correct aperture had been set.

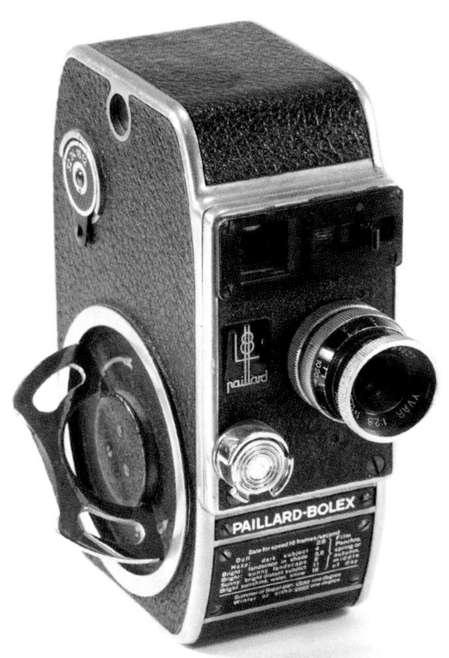

In 1946 Bolex, previously best known for large 16 mm and 8 mm cameras, introduced its first 8 mm compact design. The L8 offered interchangeable lenses, viewfinder masks for their different views, a range of shooting speeds and a film-end warning in the viewfinder.

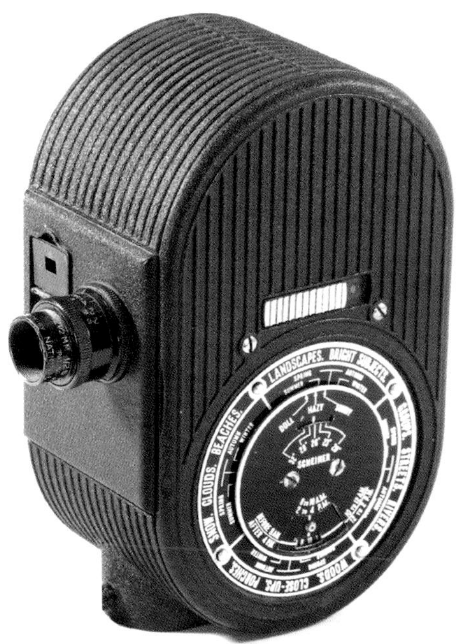

Dekko's first 8 mm camera in 1947 took on an oval-shaped die-cast black metal body. It could be adapted with a special accessory for reflex viewing before shooting.

The three-lens turret previously seen on 16 mm cameras soon began to make an appearance on Standard-8 cameras, and it became commonplace for each lens to have its own viewfinder, rotated into position as the lens was changed. Some cameras incorporated a second viewfinder that looked through the lens next to the one in the shooting position for accurate focusing before twisting that lens into place.

One of the earliest 8 mm cameras to feature a built-in photo-electric exposure meter was the Nizo Heliomatic Model S2R, made in 1952. It featured a turret for two lenses plus an extra space for a lens-shaped exposure meter with a photo-electric cell where the front element would normally be found on a lens. All

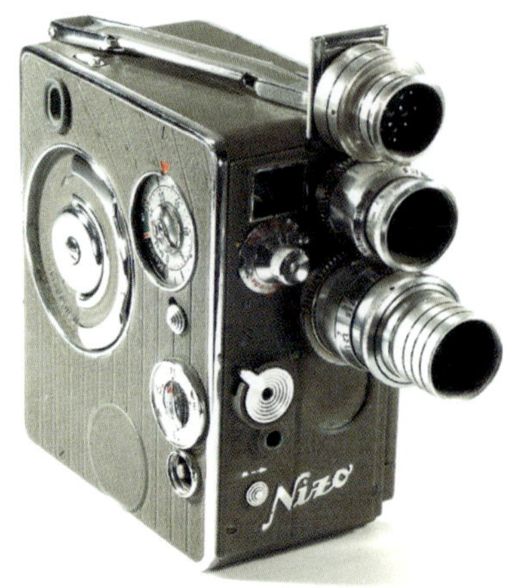

The Nizo Heliomat S2R was claimed, in 1952, to be one of the first with a built-in photo-electric photocell meter, which was incorporated into a sliding turret that also contained two lenses. A similar lens-styled meter, mounted in a rotating turret, was used in the Sankyo 8E around 1960.

three were mounted in a straight line, one above the other. The iris diaphragms of the two lenses were geared together and similarly coupled to another iris in front of the meter cell. As lens apertures were opened and closed, a moving needle swung across the viewfinder to line up with a second needle, indicating that exposure had been correctly set.

Early zoom lenses, such as the Pan Cinor, which allowed a seamless adjustment from wide-angle to telephoto in a single lens, began to appear as add-on accessories around this time. They came equipped with their own reflex viewing system, which enabled the photographer to look through the actual camera lens rather than through a separate eyepiece. Eventually

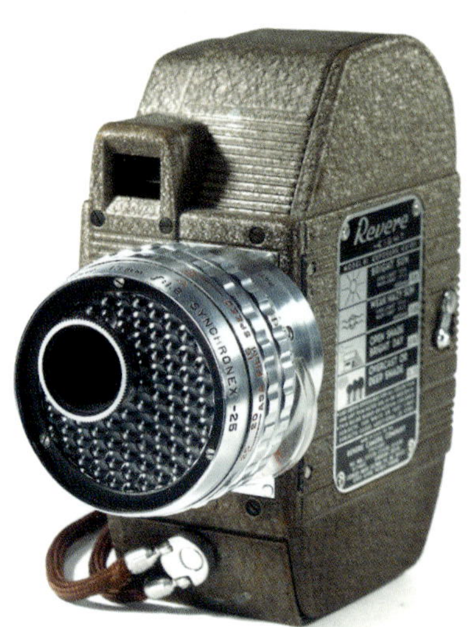

Left: *The Elgeet Synchronex 8 was a lens combined with a surrounding meter, sold as an accessory to fit cameras without built-in meters. It is seen here fitted to a Revere Ranger-8 from the late 1950s.*

Below: *Between 1953 and 1959 Zeiss introduced a range of unusually shaped 8 mm cameras in which the film ran horizontally through the body, with a twist in the middle as it passed through the film gate. Produced with different specifications and at least one variation of body colour, these were the Movikon and Movinette cameras.*

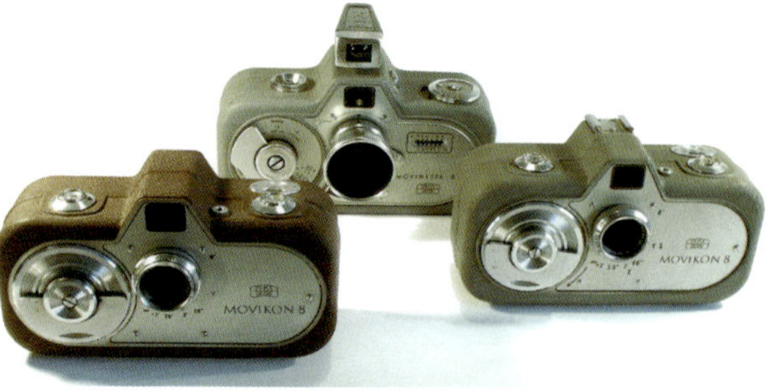

Right: *Parallax – the difference between the view seen by the lens and that from the viewfinder – was often compensated for by tilting viewfinders, seen here on the LD-8, made by Pierre Leveque in 1953, and later on the Admira 8F, made by Meopta in 1960.*

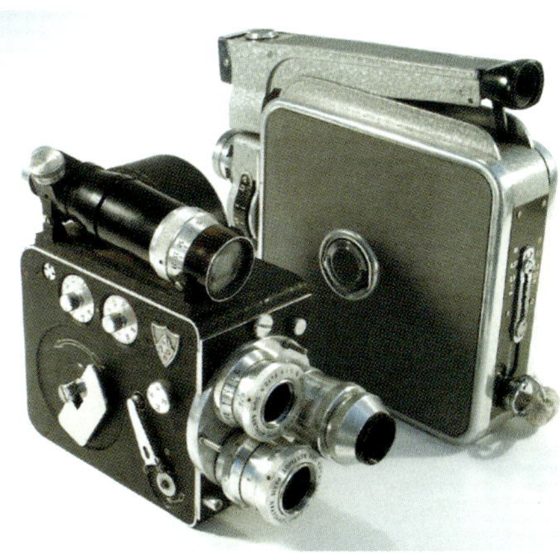

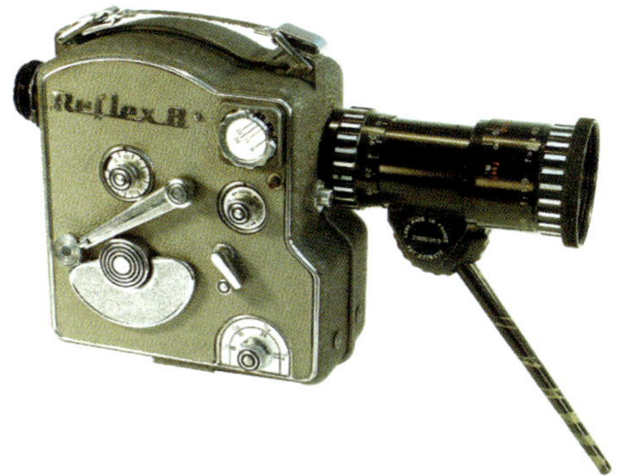

Above: *Reflex viewfinding, which allowed the viewfinder to look through the lens during filming, was first seen on an 8 mm camera with the Camex, made by Ercsam in 1956. It utilised a mirror on the back of the shutter, which reflected light to the viewfinder only when the shutter was closed, which produced an annoying flickering effect as the film advanced.*

Right: *A better reflex system came with the Pan Cinor lens, which did away with the flickering effect by using a beam splitter to send light to film and viewfinder at the same time. By the end of the 1950s such lenses were being sold as accessories for non-reflex 8 mm cameras complete with their own attached viewfinders. One is seen here on a Bolex B8L.*

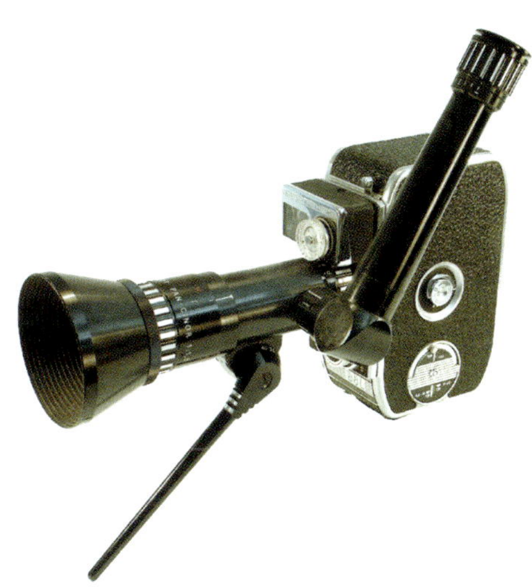

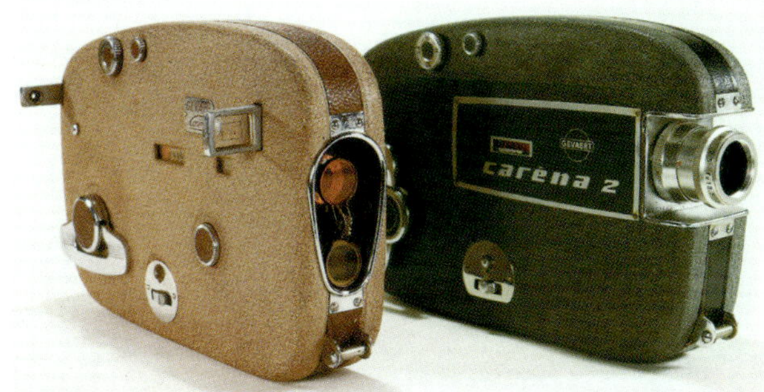

These two very stylish 8 mm cameras were made in 1954 and 1955 by the Carena factory in Switzerland. The first and second models, made in brown and green respectively, attained their ultra-slimline design by the positioning of the motor behind the film spools.

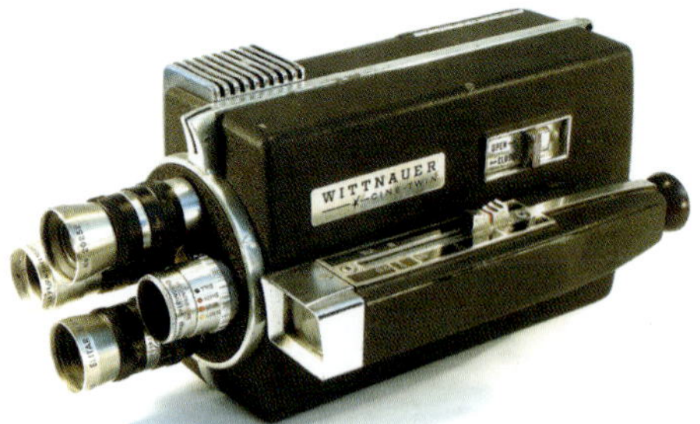

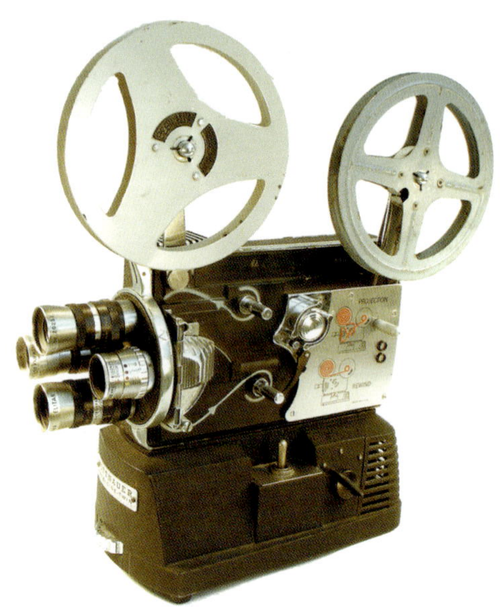

The American Wittnauer company in 1957 resurrected the old idea of combining a camera and a projector with the Cine-Twin. The camera was battery-driven and had four lenses on its turret, only three of which were for filming. The fourth lens came into play for projection when the camera was mounted on a special base that plugged into mains electricity to power a 400 watt projector bulb incorporated into the body. With the side of the camera removed, arms folded up to accommodate 300 foot (91 metre) reels of Standard-8 film.

zooms became the normal standard lens for all but the cheapest cine cameras. Reflex viewfinding, built into the body of the camera, arrived in the Standard-8 format with the French Camex Reflex-8 in 1956.

In 1958 a new attempt at reviving the Single-8 gauge was attempted with the Bolsey-8, but the idea failed again. In the same year Bell & Howell introduced the Autoset, whose meter

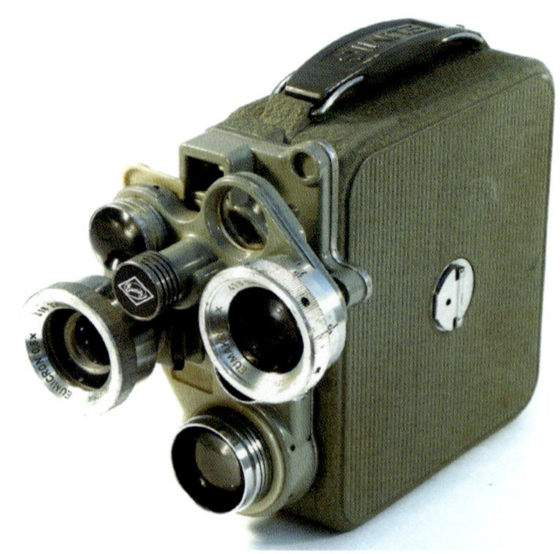

The Eumig C3R of 1958 loaded its turret up with five lenses – three for shooting and two that changed the view through the viewfinder as the telephoto or wide-angle lens adaptor was turned into position.

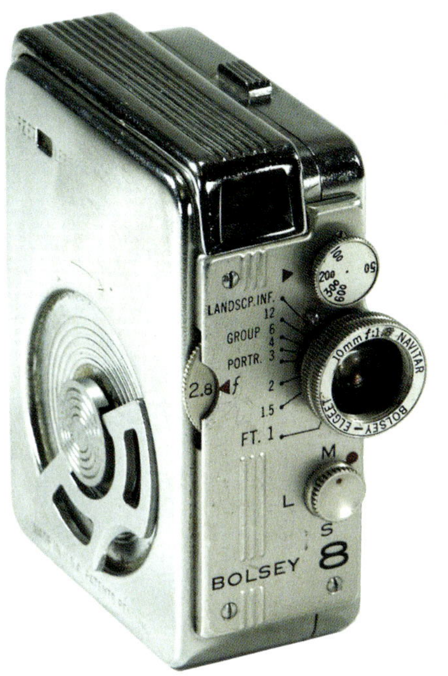

The Bolsey-8, made in 1958 and advertised as the world's smallest cine camera, used its own unique cartridge of 8 mm film and was unusual in doubling as a true subminiature still camera with a full range of shutter speeds.

was coupled to the aperture control to set exposures automatically. At the same time Bolex introduced the B8L, whose built-in meter took its reading directly through the lens for even more accurate exposure setting.

In the 1960s some Standard-8 cameras began to take on new slimline bodies, with electric motors now taking over from clockwork. Others, such as those from the Japanese Sekonic

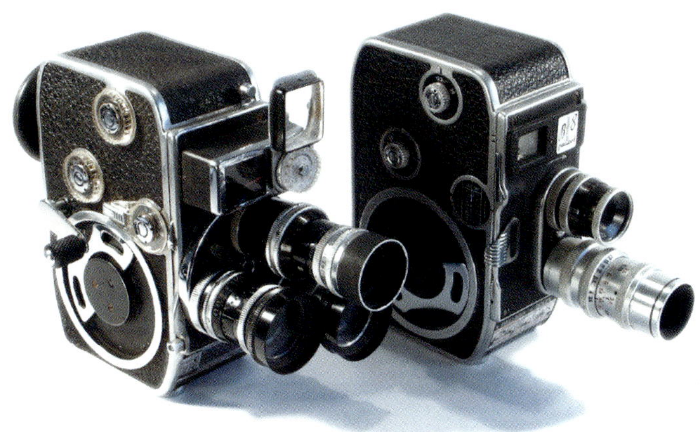

The compact-size Bolex cameras came with many varying specifications, incorporating two- and three-lens turrets. These two models are the B8 from 1953 and the D8L from 1959.

The Eumig Servomatic, made in 1960, was the first 8 mm camera to offer fully automatic exposure control.

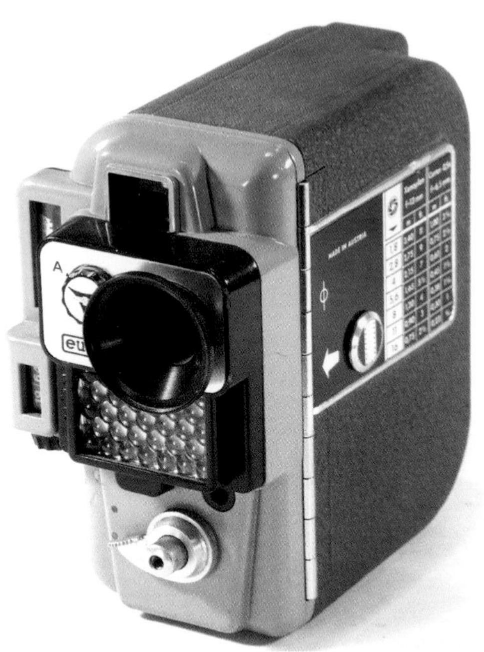

factory, introduced new features such as the flip-over body that offered a way of turning the film over for its second run through the camera without actually removing it from the body.

By now the Japanese had started to make serious inroads into the photographic world. In 1961 Japanese production of amateur cine cameras

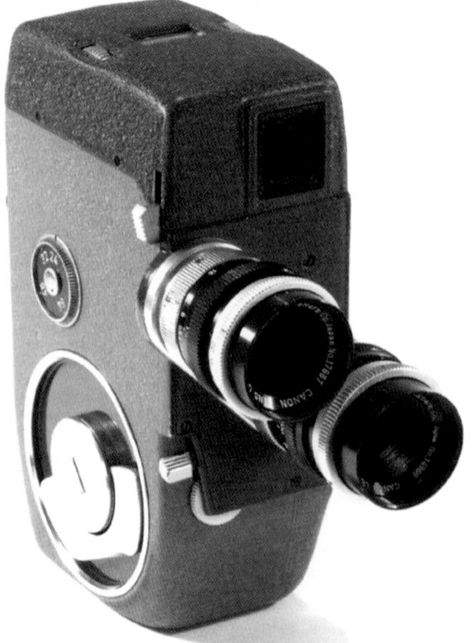

Canon was among the first of the Japanese manufacturers to break into the Western world of amateur cine. This early model is the Canon 8 from 1958.

The Leicina 8S, introduced in 1960, was an 8 mm camera from Leitz, better known for its high-quality 35 mm still cameras. It used a fixed standard lens that could be adapted for wide-angle or telephoto shooting. The company continued to make cine cameras for the later Super-8 gauge, but was out of the cine business by 1975.

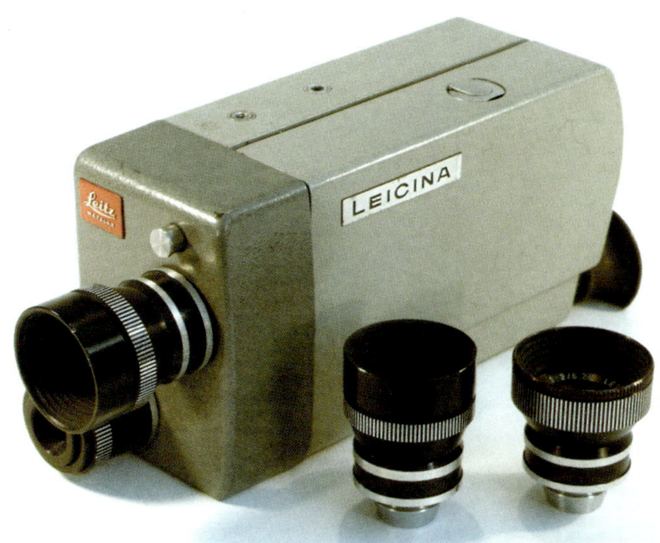

totalled 685,000, of which 98 per cent were 8 mm models. The figure showed an increase of 15 per cent on the previous year, of which around 70 per cent were exported, an increase of 12 per cent in quantity and 32 per cent in value. This high figure was attributed mainly to new features including automatic exposure and zoom lenses as standard.

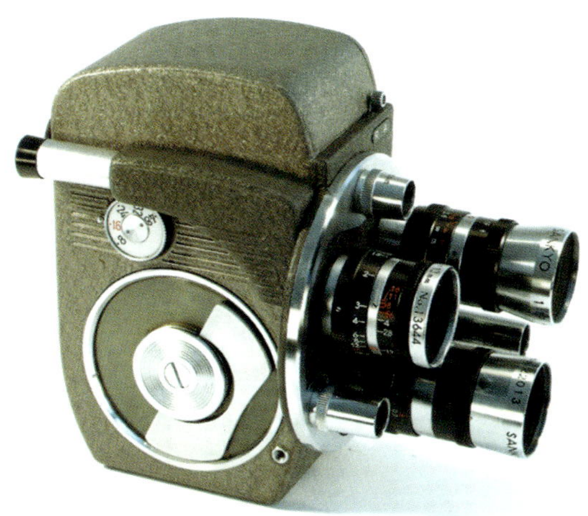

The Sankyo 8-R from 1960 incorporated twin viewfinders – one for normal filming and a second that looked through the lens adjacent to the one in the shooting position, to check in advance for critical focus.

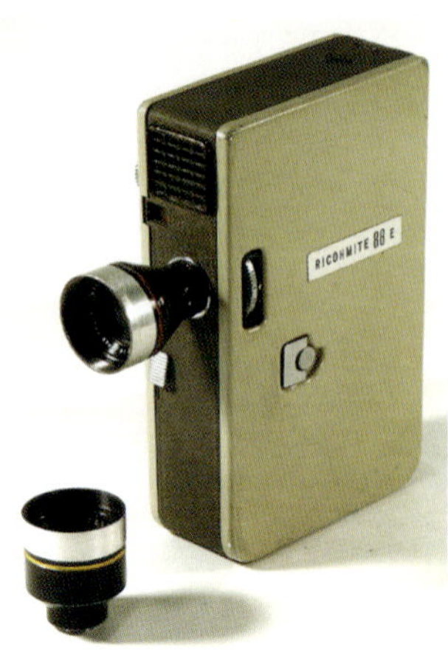

Right: *The Japanese Ricomite 88E was a slimline pocket camera from 1963, which offered semi-automatic exposure and lens adaptors to convert the standard lens for wide-angle or telephoto.*

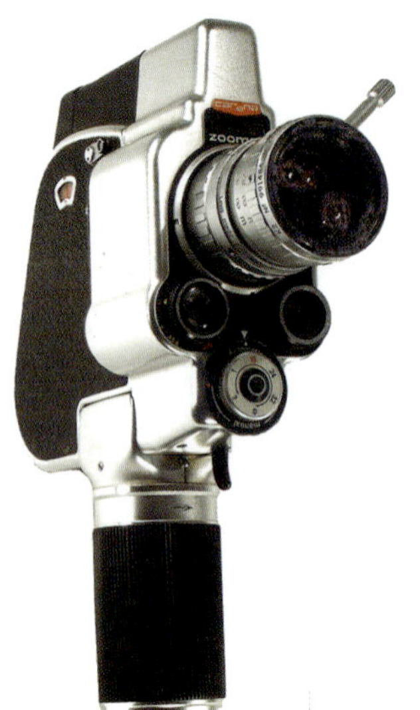

Above: *The Carena Zoomex, made in 1961, achieved its unusual and stylish look by incorporating its clockwork motor into the handle, which was twisted to wind the spring.*

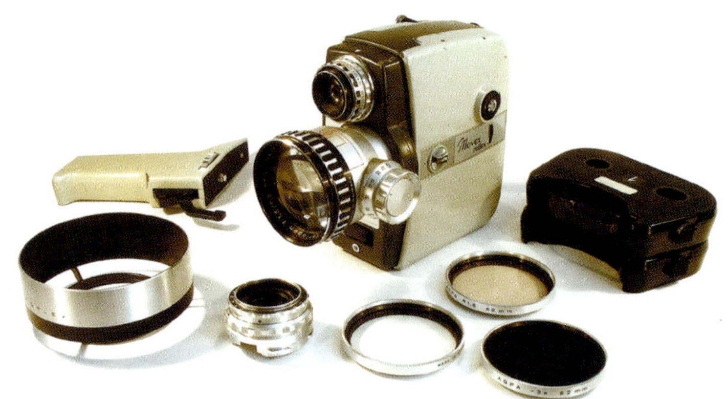

Above: *The Agfa Movex Reflex, launched in 1963, took normal Standard-8 film or cartridges. It was sold as a complete system that included a close-up converter lens, spare cartridges, pistol grip, filters and lens hood.*

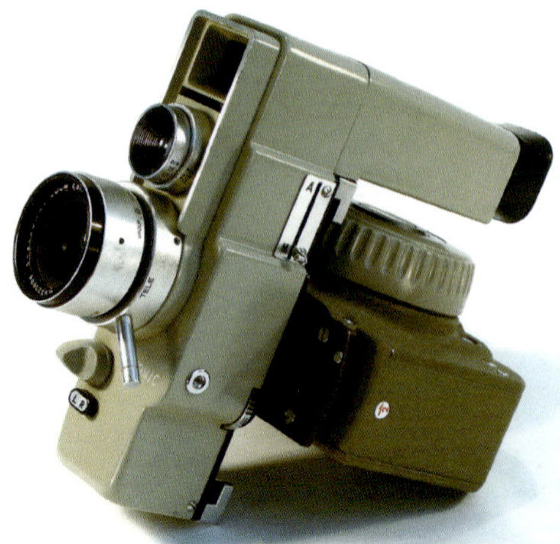

Left: *The Sankyo company introduced a series of cameras that allowed Standard-8 film to be reversed after the first run by flipping the part of the body that contained the film spools through 180 degrees. This model is the Dualmatic Zoom from 1963.*

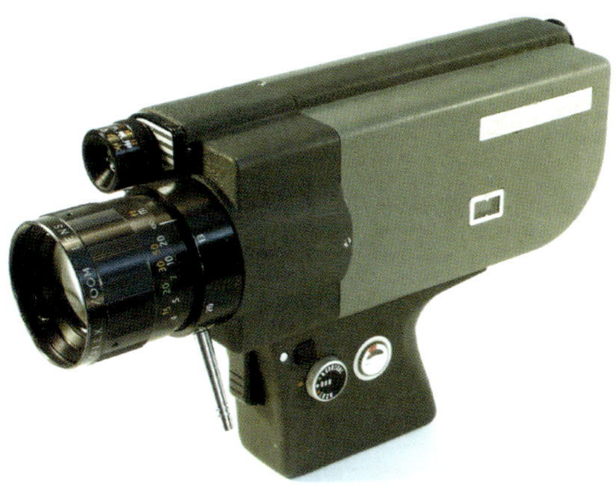

Typical of the new streamlined look that came to some Standard-8 cameras at the end of their reign, this is the Concorde from the Japanese Chinon factory in 1964.

Right: *Minolta's Minoltina came right at the end of the Standard-8 era, in 1965, just as Super-8 was being launched. It took pre-loaded film cartridges and featured a slim body with fold-down grip that doubled as a lens protector.*

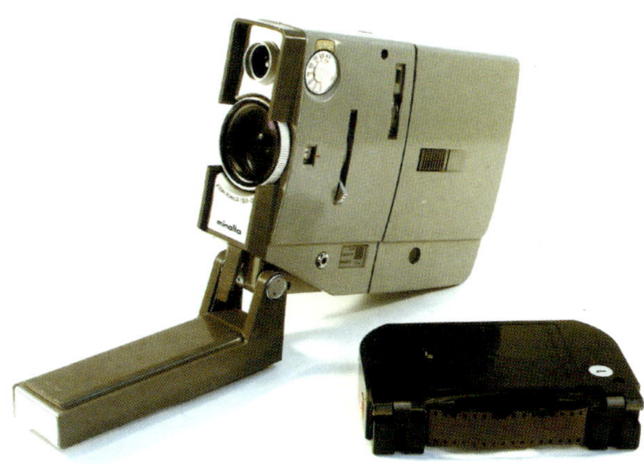

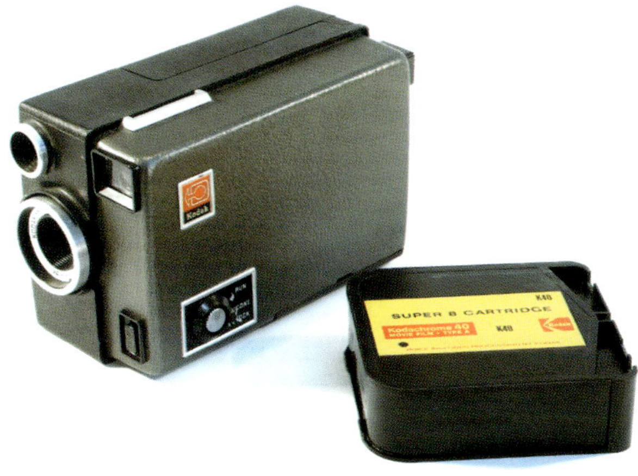

The Instamatic M4 was one of the first Super-8 cameras, launched by Kodak in 1965, along with the similar but simpler M2 model.

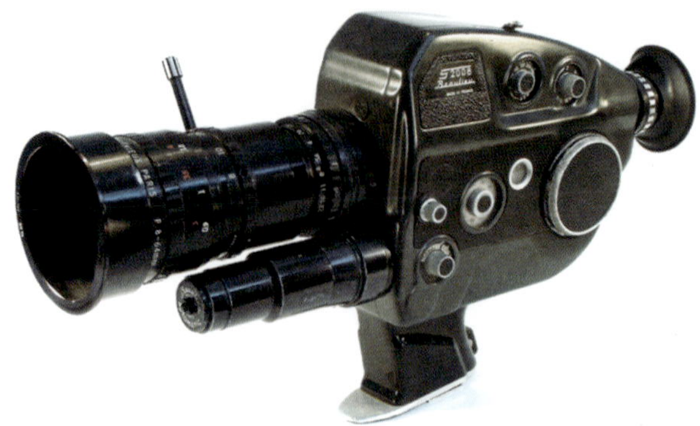

Left: *In 1966, only one year after the introduction of Super-8, the Beaulieu 2008S took on a streamlined design in a camera that offered automatic exposure and a range of sophisticated features rarely seen before in amateur equipment.*

Right: *Fuji's stylish challenge to Kodak's Super-8 gauge, as seen in the Fujica P-1 and P-300. It was the last time the Single-8 system would be tried.*

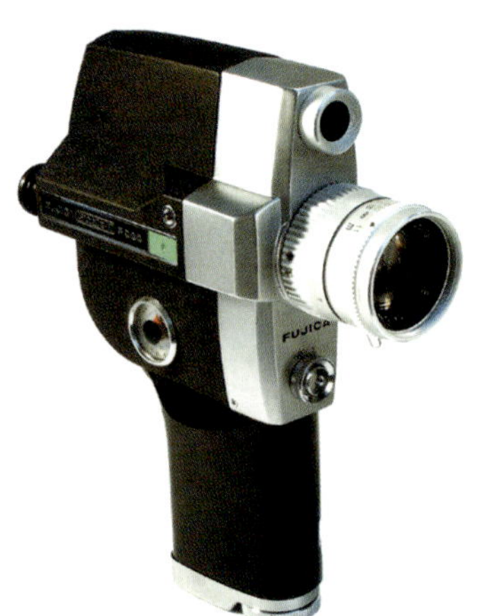

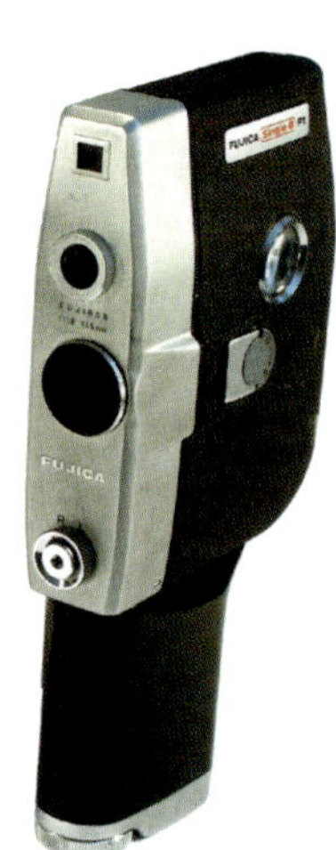

At this point, Kodak did it again. With Standard-8 cameras about as sophisticated as it was possible to get for the amateur, the photographic giant introduced a new version in 1965. This time it was called 'Super-8', characterised by easy-to-use cameras and film that came pre-loaded in injection-moulded plastic cartridges, 50 feet (15 metres) in length. It ran through the camera only once. Still 8 mm wide, the film utilised smaller sprocket holes and gave an increased image size.

Within a year the new format had a challenger in the shape of Fuji in Japan, who once again revived the Single-8 gauge in a short-lived series of small, compact and – compared to the early Kodak models – very stylish cameras. The Fuji Single-8 system was probably better than Kodak's Super-8, but only Ilford seriously followed Fuji's lead, and only for a very short while. Eventually Single-8 died away for the last time.

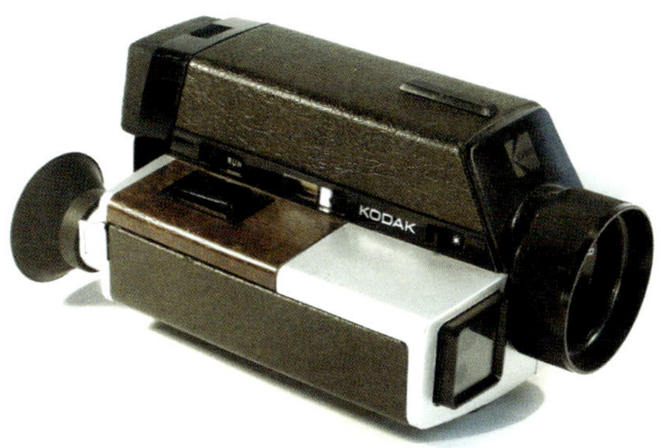

The Kodak XL33 Super-8 camera launched in 1971 took a very different approach to cine-camera design in a fully automatic model.

Super-8, by comparison, went from strength to strength with cameras becoming more sophisticated, zoom lenses offering greater ranges and even sound on film becoming a reality for the amateur, not for the first time, but certainly in the most successful way to date. Super-8 remained the gauge for the serious amateur until the decline of cine photography as a hobby in the 1980s.

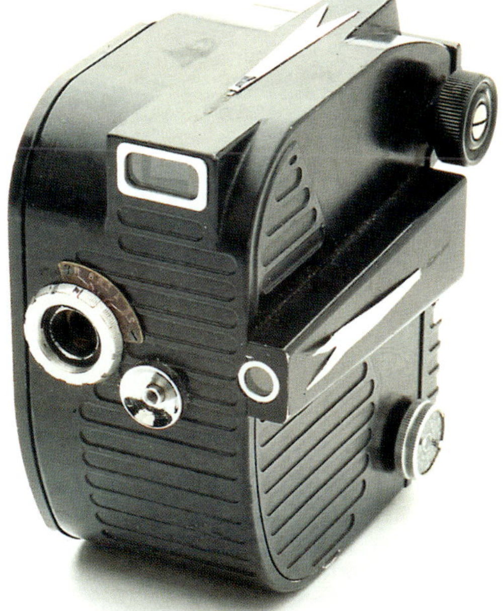

The Janus, made in Russia during the early 1960s, was unique in being a cine camera and still camera combined. It had two lenses and shutters, situated on each side of the body, with a separate viewfinder for each, and took two different films in the same body – Standard-8 for movies and 35 mm for stills.

Professional influences

While amateur cine cameras pursued the route to lower costs with narrower film gauges, the professional world, with its higher budgets, stuck primarily to 35 mm. In theory the working of those professional cameras was similar to their amateur counterparts, albeit on a larger scale, but certain innovations that came early to professional cameras took much longer to filter their way down to the amateur market.

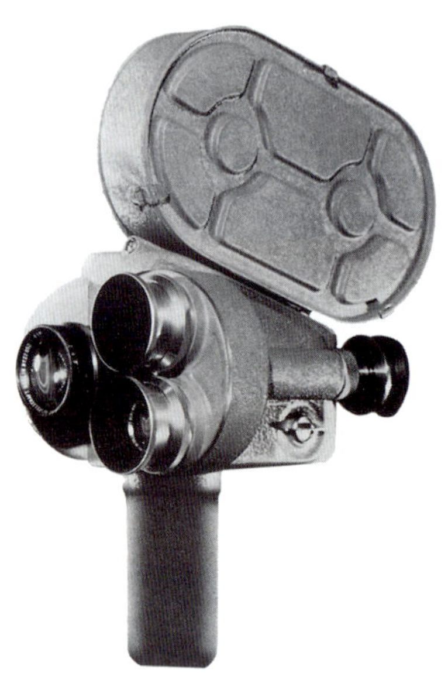

Reflex viewfinding is a prime example. Although, as already noted, it was 1956 before the technology came to the amateur, it had previously been introduced into professional 35 mm cameras with the Arriflex 35 way back in 1937.

Perhaps the biggest difference between professional and amateur equipment lay in their approaches to adding sound. Right from the start, Thomas Edison saw moving images not as an end in themselves but as an adjunct to his previous invention, the phonograph, patented in 1877. As early as 1894, in his Black Maria studio, he

Left and below: *The Arriflex 35, made in 1937 for 35 mm film, was the first commercially produced camera with a reflex viewfinder system, a technology that did not arrive in 16 mm cameras until 1952, with the Arriflex 16ST. It would still be a few years more before the technology came to amateur cameras.*

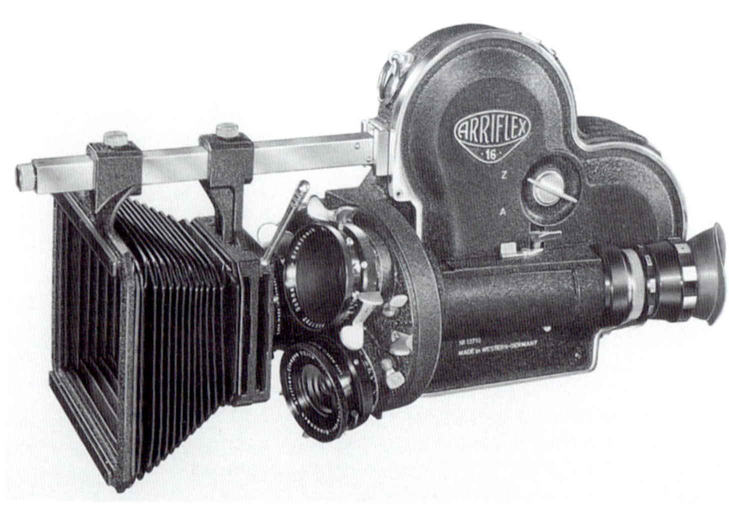

attempted to record sound on a phonograph cylinder simultaneously with shooting film, and in 1895 he introduced the Kinetophone, which supplied a musical accompaniment to his Kinetoscope films.

In 1902 French pioneer Leon Gaumont introduced the Chronophone, which coupled a single projector to two phonographs using a special device to keep sound and vision in synchronisation. The idea was soon taken up by at least one major American film studio.

When the gramophone superseded the phonograph, putting sound on discs rather than cylinders, sound recording gained in quality and volume, and the AT&T company in the United States introduced a complete sound on disc system in 1924. This in turn led to the Vitaphone system used by Warner Brothers for the 1927 film that has come to be accepted as the first 'talkie' to hit commercial cinemas. Called *The Jazz Singer*, it starred Al Jolson and was essentially a silent film with only the musical numbers and a few of Jolson's ad-libs actually reaching the soundtrack.

The main problem with these early systems was synchronisation. Vision and sound were shot and recorded separately, only coming together as the film was projected, and although sound systems have always had to run at a constant speed to prevent distortion, projectors are notorious for running at slightly varying speeds. As a result, sound and vision inevitably drifted apart.

Synchronisation became more accurate with the introduction of optical recording. This involved converting variations in sound to a photographic image exposed on to the side of the film. Discussed in theory as early as 1900, it eventually became a reality in the same year as the release of *The Jazz Singer*, when the Fox studios adopted the technology and set out to film and record vaudeville acts with their Movitone system. Warner Brothers, however, had already signed up many of the popular acts of the day, so Fox used the new technology instead to make the first sound newsreels. Optical sound technology was installed in most movie theatres by the end of the 1930s.

An early attempt at incorporating the sound-recording equipment into a camera came from the Radio Corporation of America (RCA) in 1933. The camera was a 16 mm model with a microphone fitted into the back. With the camera to his eye, the cameraman could then speak his commentary into the microphone while shooting. As he did so, a tiny acoustically coupled mirror reflected a beam of light to expose an optical soundtrack on to the edge of a single-perforated film.

In 1932 Pathé resurrected the 17.5 mm gauge and in 1934 added an optical soundtrack to it, though not with the degree of success that would have made it a commercial proposition. The French company even tried its hand at adding optical sound to 9.5 mm films.

With the advent of recording sound on magnetic tape, first demonstrated in 1935 and further developed during the Second World War years of 1939–45, domestic tape recorders soon introduced a new way for professionals and then amateurs to add sound to film. In the amateur world, the two could be synchronised by the use of special devices that mechanically monitored the movement of tape spools and projector reels, comparing them and using an electrical connection to speed up or slow down the projector as necessary.

A better method of synchronisation came from adding a magnetic stripe of iron oxide to the film itself, enabling the recording of sound directly on to film. Very few manufacturers, however, considered the potential for magnetic stripe recording during actual filming. More often, the film would be shot silently, then the magnetic stripe added after processing, with the soundtrack recorded and played back by the projector. The exception was the American Fairchild Company, which produced the Cinephonic range of cameras that took not only normal Standard-8 film but also the company's own pre-striped version of 8 mm in 100 foot (30 metre) reels.

By the 1950s, 16 mm cameras were beginning to be used in the

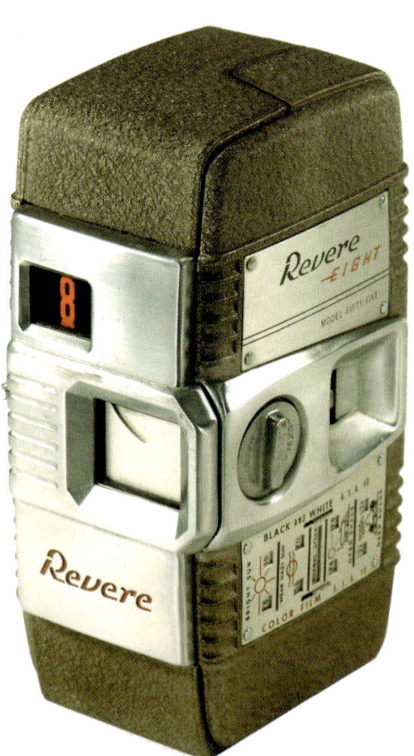

Professional techniques such as fades between shots were brought to the amateur market with the Revere Eight Model 55 in 1950, which incorporated an opening and closing shutter for the purpose in front of the lens.

Professional effects on amateur equipment could be attained with accessories such as this clockwork-driven Bolsey Cine-fader, seen attached to a Bell & Howell Model 605 from 1951.

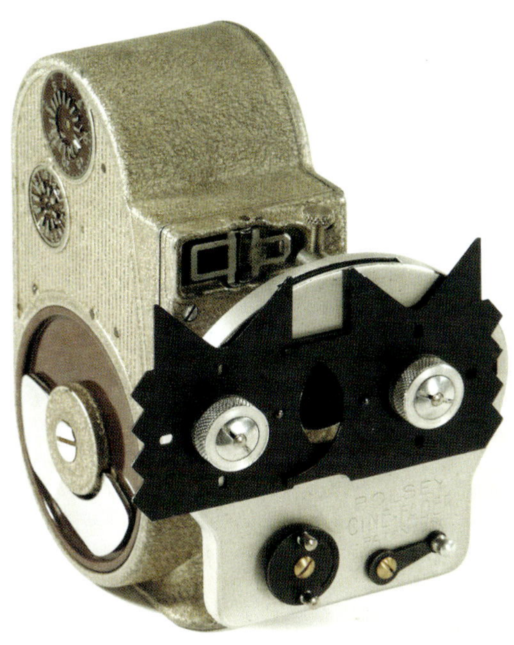

professional world of television, advertising and newsreels, and some adopted the magnetic stripe technology to add sound. In the big film studios, however, 35 mm cameras and optical sound dominated, although by now it had become apparent that, for reasons of quality and ease of editing, it made sense to use separate equipment for sound recording and film shooting, combining the two later by transferring the soundtrack optically to the side of the film. Synchronisation during shooting was maintained via an electronic link that placed a regular pulse, emitted by the camera, on to the recording medium. To prevent the sound of the

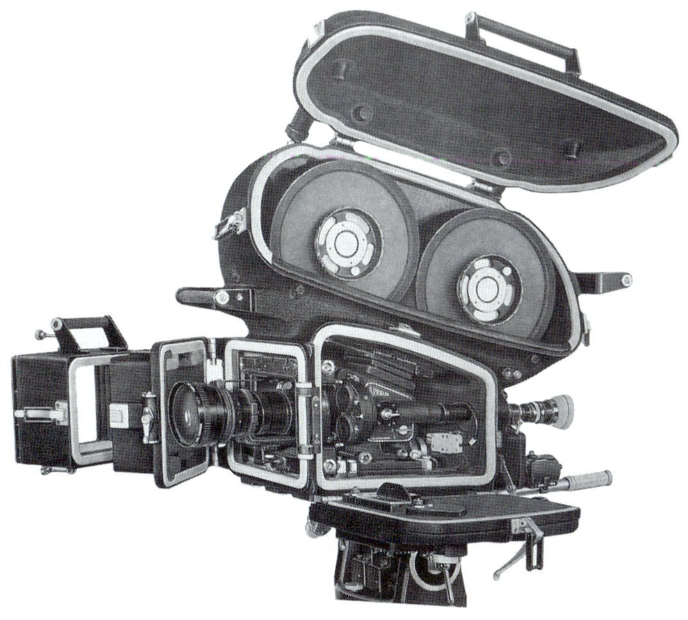

The first blimps were made in the 1950s to sound-proof 16 mm and 35 mm professional cameras so that sound could safely be recorded separately from the camera.

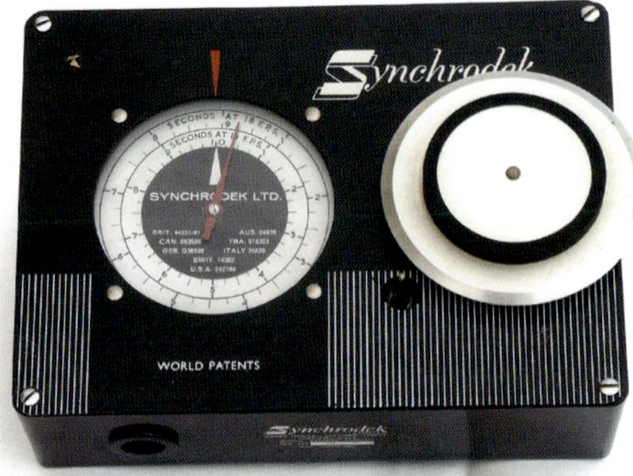

The Synchrodek provided a mechanical and electrical link between a tape recorder and a projector, resulting in a fairly accurate method of retaining synchronisation between the two.

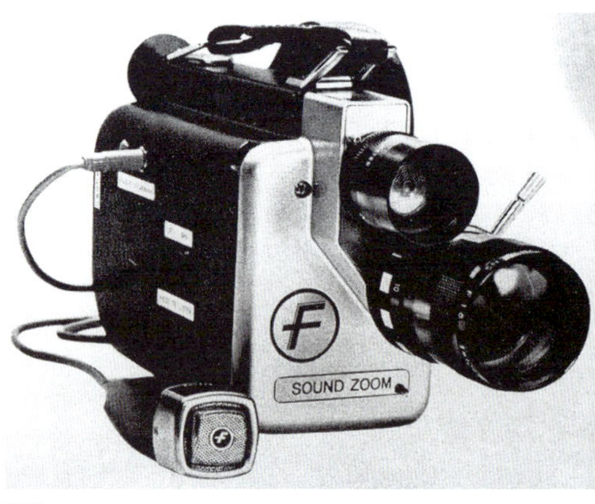

The Cinephonic 902, made by Fairchild in the United States in 1963, was an unusual attempt at shooting sound and vision together, using special pre-striped 8 mm film.

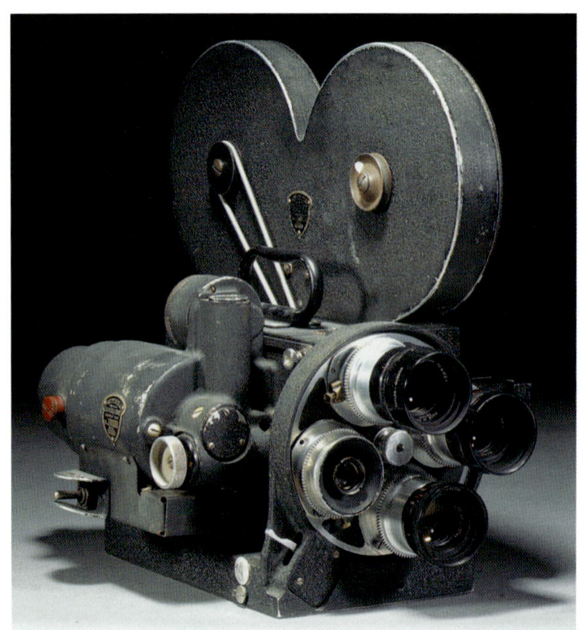

By 1960 16 mm, which started as an amateur gauge, had been adopted by many professional film makers, especially those working in television, using cameras such as this Mitchell 16, made by the Mitchell Camera Corporation in California.

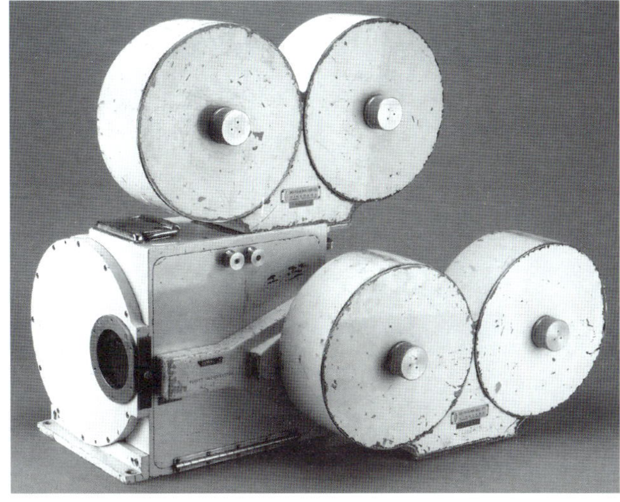

A Cinerama camera from 1960. This model was made to take 65 mm film and superseded the original idea of shooting on three interlocked cameras.

camera being recorded on to the soundtrack, the cameras were covered in sound-proof units, known as 'blimps'.

The popularisation of amateur sound films only became a reality with the introduction of Super-8, and Kodak soon introduced a range of Super-8 films already striped for recording in a new generation of cameras. The system was called Single System Sound, and by the 1970s it was the norm for amateur use.

Single System Sound cameras had built-in circuitry to record the sound direct, via a microphone that could be extended on a telescopic boom from a point above the lens. International standards regarding the separation between the recording head and the film gate were established to ensure that sound film would replay on any Super-8 projector.

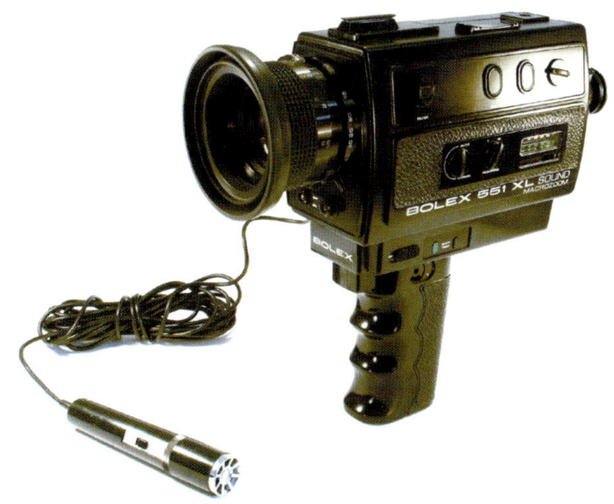

Amateur sound finally became a reality with cameras such as the Bolex 551 XL, made during the 1970s. The camera recorded sound via its own directional microphone plugged into the side of the body. An earpiece or headphones could also be plugged in to monitor the sound as the film was shot. The camera was fully automatic, with a reflex viewfinder, power zoom, fade-in/fade-out control and macro focusing.

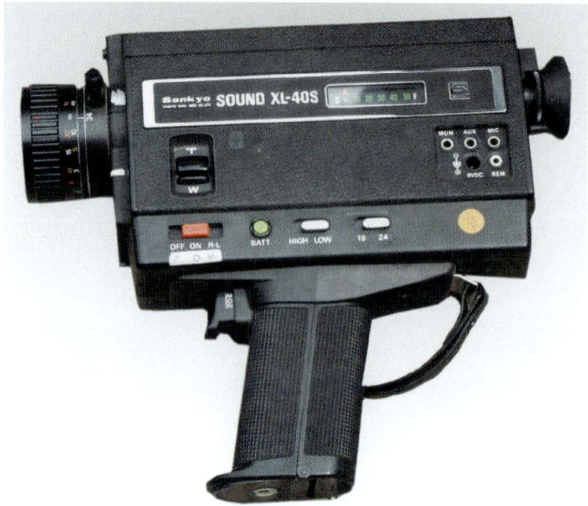

Before long, amateur sound became the norm even on budget-priced Japanese Super-8 cameras such as this Sankyo Sound XL-40S.

The mechanics of a sound camera were only slightly different from those of a silent one, the main difference involving the jerking movement that takes any film through a cine camera gate. The flow of the stripe – and therefore the film – needed to be more even over the recording heads, so a second, constant-speed, motor was incorporated. This allowed the film to be gripped between a capstan and a pressure roller while a constant eighteen-frame gap between picture and sound was maintained by a loop sensor that acted as a signalling device to the camera's main drive. This responded by very slightly increasing or decreasing its speed to keep the picture in constant step with the sound.

So sound finally came to amateur film making. Whether or not optical sound would ever have reached amateur equipment is debatable. There is evidence that Kodak was researching into adding optical sound to Super-8 films as early as 1966, the year after the new gauge was launched. But it never happened, and by the middle of the 1970s interest in amateur cine cameras was seriously waning.

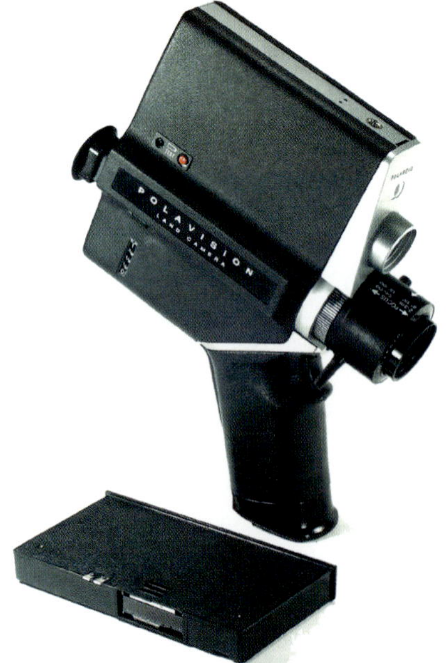

Towards the end of the cine era, several manufacturers tried to launch new ideas to revive the hobby. In 1977 Polaroid introduced Polavision, which took a special film that incorporated processing chemicals in its cartridge. Placing the cartridge in the system's viewer after shooting rewound the film for viewing and processed it at the same time.

In the professional world the situation was markedly different, as a buoyant film industry, boosted by the introduction of multiplex cinemas in the last years of the twentieth century, meant that equipment continued to be made and improved upon.

Not that every innovation in professional cine equipment was a success. Some systems that seemed to be amazing innovations in their time vanished within a few years of their launch. Cinerama, first seen in 1952, was originally shot on three synchronised cameras side by side before being projected on to a curved screen by three interlocked projectors. Later, the name was retained for a less ambitious system that used 65 mm film in a single camera. Vista Vision in 1953 ran the film sideways through the camera to record a larger and wider image on film for projection in specially designed projectors, or printed on to a normal-width 35 mm frame for projection in conventional equipment. Todd-AO in 1954 used special cameras that took 65 mm wide film in place of 35 mm. It was then printed on to 75 mm wide film for projection purposes.

Without attaining any long-lasting success in the professional world, none of these systems had any effect on amateur cine equipment. On the other hand, widescreen, as popularised by CinemaScope in 1953, did attain professional acceptance and even found a place in the hearts of some specialist amateur film makers. This was chiefly because it used special lenses rather than any new form of camera or projector. Known as 'anamorphic' lenses, these squeezed the image at the shooting stage and expanded it again in the projector, a technique that could be applied to amateur equipment almost as easily as professional. Likewise, the craze for three-dimensional films that came and went in the professional cinema during the 1950s also swept through the amateur world. Sound in particular underwent a metamorphosis in professional film making in the 1980s with the introduction of systems such as Dolby.

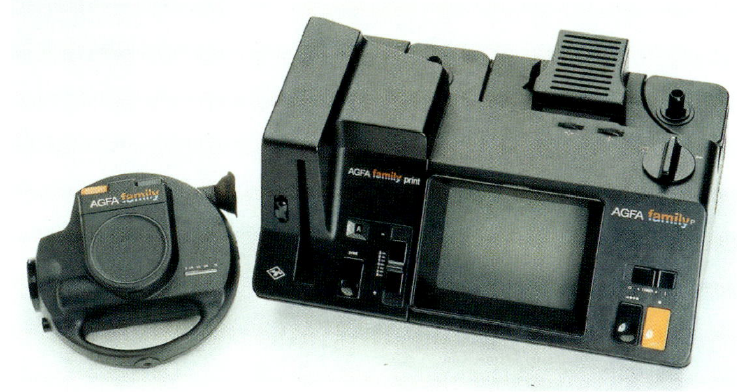

Agfa's answer to the failing cine market in 1980 came with the Family Camera, which took movie and still images on Super-8 film. Shown on the system's own viewer, individual frames could be paused and an instant print made, using Kodak's now defunct instant photography system.

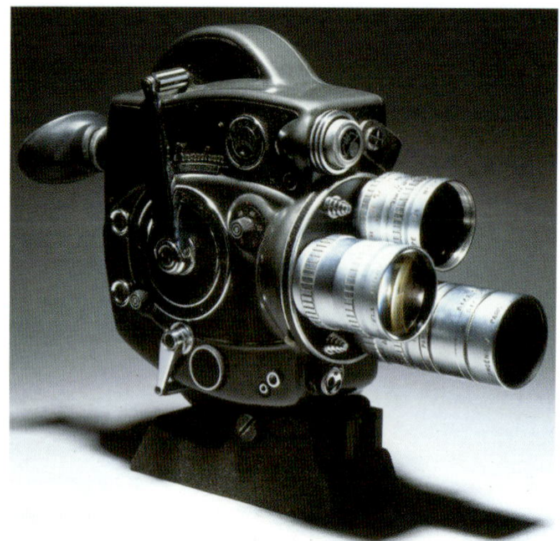

In 1961 the Beaulieu R16 fell right on the boundary between amateur and professional equipment. Although a camera such as this would have been used predominantly by professional film makers, the company also produced the R9.5, with the same body but made to take 9.5 mm film, which a few amateurs were still using even at this late stage.

Below left: *In 1989 the Arriflex 765 was the first compact, light and silent 65 mm production camera with a reflex viewfinder.*

Below right: *The digital age of professional cameras, represented by the DDW-F900 camera, made by Sony and modified by Panavision following the collaboration of the two companies in 1997. Cameras such as this were used to film the second wave of 'Star Wars' films.*

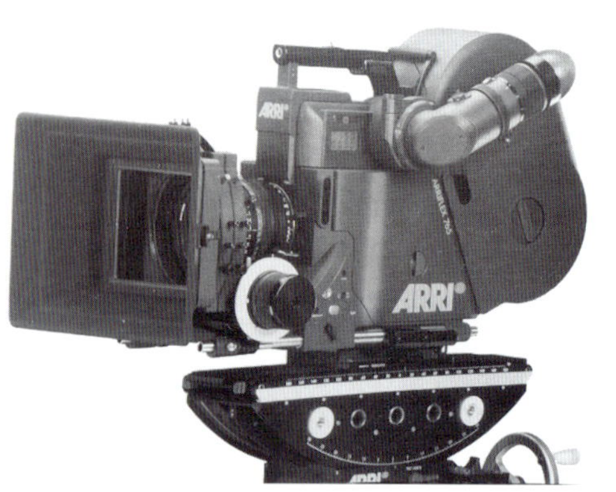

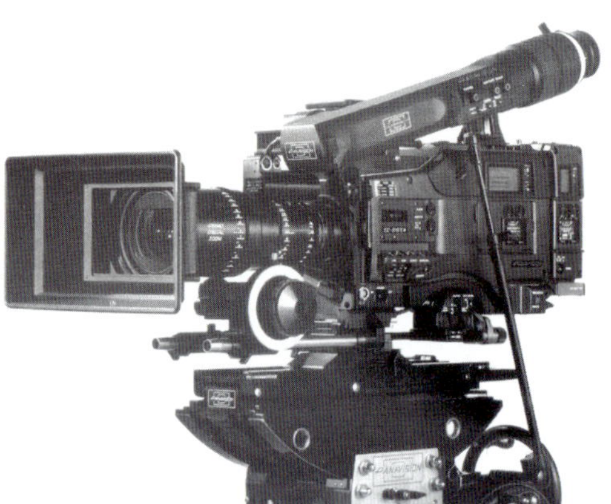

But, by and large, professional innovations such as these left the amateur cine-camera world behind. By the mid 1980s amateur cinematography was a thing of the past for all but a minority of die-hard enthusiasts. With video already making inroads into the amateur world, manufacturers simply stopped making the cameras. For many, this signalled the end of film making as a hobby and, for the amateur market at least, the end of a long and illustrious line of cine cameras.

Further information

Books

Coe, Brian. *The History of Movie Photography.* Ash & Grant, 1981. Out of print but worth seeking out second-hand.

Lossau, Jürgen. *Filmkameras (Movie Cameras).* Atol Medien, 2000. Printed in English and German.

Lothrop, Eaton, and Spira, S. F. *The History of Photography as Seen through the Spira Collection.* Aperture, 2002. Mostly covers still equipment but includes a major chapter on cine.

Wade, John. *The Collector's Guide to Cine Cameras.* Hove Books, 2001. Devoted mainly to collecting amateur equipment.

Club

The Photographic Collectors Club of Great Britain. While most members are still-camera collectors, there is a small contingent interested in cine. Contact the membership secretary at 5 Buntingford Road, Puckeridge, Ware, Hertfordshire SG11 1RT. Telephone: 01920 821611. Website: www.pccgb.org

Museums

Kingston Museum, Wheatfield Way, Kingston, Surrey KT1 2PS. Telephone: 020 8546 5386. Website: www.kingston.gov.uk/museum Includes a gallery on pre-cinema and the birth of movies, including the work of Eadweard Muybridge.

Leeds Industrial Museum, Armley Mills, Canal Road, Armley, Leeds LS12 2QF. Telephone: 0113 263 7861. Website: www.leeds.gov.uk/armleymills Has displays of movie cameras and projectors, as well as a recreation of a 1920s cinema.

Life In A Lens, 118 North Parade, Matlock Bath, Derbyshire DE4 3NS. Telephone: 01629 583325. Website: www.lifeinalens.co.uk Privately owned museum that traces the complete history of photography in various themed rooms. Contains a small amount of cine equipment.

The National Museum of Photography, Film and Television, Bradford, West Yorkshire BD1 1NQ. Telephone: 0870 701 0200. Website: www.nmpft.org.uk This is the largest British museum of its kind and it contains a major section on amateur and professional movie equipment.

The Science Museum, Exhibition Road, South Kensington, London SW7 2DD. Telephone: 0870 870 4868. Website: www.sciencemuseum.org.uk Covers all sciences, including a gallery on movie equipment.

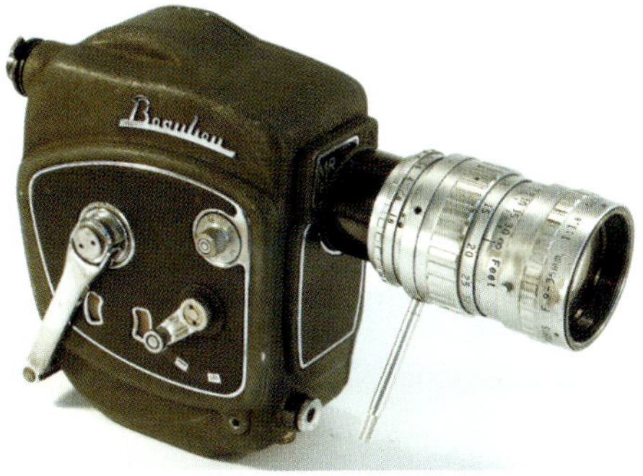

By the 1960s zoom lenses were becoming standard on most 8 mm cameras. This one is on the Beaulieu MR8, which also offered reflex viewing.

Index